Broken

But Some Pieces Still Work

By

Dr. Jerlette Mickie

authorHOUSE™

1663 Liberty Drive, Suite 200
Bloomington, Indiana 47403
(800) 839-8640
www.AuthorHouse.com

This book is a work of non-fiction. Unless otherwise noted, the author and the publisher make no explicit guarantees as to the accuracy of the information contained in this book and in some cases, names of people and places have been altered to protect their privacy.

© 2005 Dr. Jerlette Mickie. All Rights Reserved.

No part of this book may be reproduced, stored in a retrieval system, or transmitted by any means without the written permission of the author.

First published by AuthorHouse 05/31/05

ISBN: 1-4208-4101-7 (e)
ISBN: 1-4208-4100-9 (sc)
ISBN: 1-4208-4102-5 (dj)

Printed in the United States of America
Bloomington, Indiana

This book is printed on acid-free paper.

DEDICATION

This book is dedicated to several people who have been influential in impacting my life, empowering my vision, raising the bar of my personality, emotions, and intellect. I can't express enough the love I hold dearest in my heart for their contributions in preparing and presenting me to the world equipped for service.

First and foremost, this book is devoted to the Lord Jesus Christ. From him I receive my inspiration and purpose for existing.

Second, it is dedicated to my beautiful and anointed wife, Leona, who has always believed in me, supported me, and walked the roads with me. I did it honey; for you said I would.

Third, I want to recognize my stepfather, Levi S. Evans to whom I owe my physical life. When my father passed when I was 7 years old, you took me and my two sisters in and gave us a roof over our head. I am forever grateful.

Fourth, I want thank my Pastor of thirty-two years, Apostle Ralph E. Green, and First Lady Shirley Green, who took me in their home and ministry and molded me into being the man I am today.

Finally, there are my three sons, Kenneth, Kevin, Korey, and daughter Sherita, all who have and continue to play a pivotal role in my life. Thanks for telling me I can do it, and that I have a global word for the nations. Thanks for helping release my dream

To my team of editors, Robert & Sherita Maxwell, for working day and night to make this book ready and available to the world; your gift and commitment to my life have been displayed in volumes. I thank you immensely!

ACKNOWLEDGEMENTS

Every meaningful adventure is often the artifact of many minds, hearts, and hands. The gifts and vigor of many such persons have gone into the creation of this book. The following individuals stand far above the rest:

- ❖ My wife, Leona, who challenged me to stop talking about writing, and provoked me into writing it down. She empowered me to stay focus and that it was time to bring the dream of writing a book to the forefront of my priorities. Without her, there would be no stories to tell and no book to write. Thanks again Leona.

- ❖ My children, who underwent timeless conversations with me, concerning what I was writing. I used them as a sounding board and editor of my thoughts. Thanks Kevin, Sherita, Yvette, Kenneth, Korey and Robert.

- ❖ My long time friends of over thirty years, Bishop Clossie and Laura Pearce, for keeping me lifted up in prayer and supporting my vision.

- ❖ To the saints of New light Cathedral for there many words of encouragement.

- ❖ To my sisters and brothers, Gail, LaFlorida, Sheila, and Tonto. Thanks for believing in me. You gave me hope.

- ❖ To my mentor, Bishop William Billy Musgrove, who found me in the projects, brushed me off, invited me to his church, and gave my life to Jesus. I am here today because of your generosity. Thanks Bishop.

Table of Contents

CHAPTER ONE BROKEN 1

CHAPTER TWO GOD HAS A DIVINE PURPOSE FOR YOU 9

CHAPTER THREE OPERATING WITH THE HURT PIECES 25

CHAPTER FOUR BROKENNESS PRESENTS AN OPPORTUNITY TO RESPOND TO GOD'S WORD 29

CHAPTER FIVE BROKEN PHYSICALLY & SPIRITUALLY 37

CHAPTER SIX STEP OVER IT, YOU CAN DO IT! 47

CHAPTER SEVEN VICTORY IN BROKENNESS 53

CHAPTER EIGHT BROKEN BUT THE VERY BEST IS COMING 61

CHAPTER NINE THE WINDS OF CORRECTION 69

CHAPTER TEN YOU WERE CREATED A WINNER 81

CHAPTER ELEVEN BROKEN THROUGH PARENTING 87

CHAPTER TWELVE SERVING MATTERS THE MOST 93

CHAPTER THIRTEEN RESHAPING OUR FRAME TO FIT HIS WILL 97

FOREWORD

As we look at the life of Job, around 1580 BC and his devoted friends, we seemingly find ourselves in the exact mindset they were in. If some unfortunate event occurs in our lives, it must have happened due to our lack of pious commitment or spiritual neglect. While we read and speak often of his story, we become just as Eliphaz, Bildad, and Zophar his dear dutiful cohorts. And, of course, later there is always an Elihu; a young, bright, and enthusiastic well-wisher who will set everyone straight with the new found insight into the situation by offering his take on the events. Elihu holds the view that the reason the situation is not any better is because the "old heads" are not willing to tell the truth and he has been given the mantle of rightness to set everyone in their place to include the "Job" that is involved.

In this book, Bishop Jerlette Mickie feverishly seeks to give us insight as to why unfortunate, heartbreaking circumstances take place in our life as he exposes himself. Is it, as supposed, that you have sinned against God or that you refuse to walk in the paths He has chosen for you? Some even have the audacity to ask, "Are you really serving Christ as you should?" The friends of Job return from history to resound their feelings again, "If you are suffering, it must be happening because you did something wrong."

I have observed many of God's people; faithful, trustworthy, honest, and full of integrity go through tragedies they have not warranted nor deserved. Yet, they remained as true as the ancient Job. "Though He slay me, yet will I trust in Him (Job 13:15a)." Today they are as committed and stalwart as ever. Their faith has not been moved, even though it seems as if they have every right to become angry, infuriated, and totally despondent to the things they have held to for so long. Yet, their walk has not wavered. They believe what mama told them is the truth, "Chil, da Lord won't leave ya!" And, this has held them together.

Being one of those persons, I believe this book addresses some of the concerns and woes of many. It wrestles with the controversy as to whether it is your inconsistency, unfaithfulness, and hidden sins or is it from other causes that you are going through this tumultuous experience. Did God really allow this to happen for your development? Bishop Mickie opens up another view to us and causes us to think what the real cause of our suffering is. He hits home when he comments that this may be a part of your destiny and God's plan for your life. It certainly does not have to come from something you did. The maxim, which states, "Good things happen to bad people and bad things happen to good people" holds true in this sense. He painstakingly tries to convey that all suffering is not because of wrong doings. Far too long we have taken this position and far too many have walked away from our faith because it has not "worked" the way it was supposed to.

The truth is outlined in these pages. Another view on why these events have taken place and visited our doorsteps may be that you are the modern day Job. Maybe God asked Satan to consider you. We always want to understand those things that are in our lives and when we do not, things become unraveled. Our worlds collide with antiquity, and like Job, we are faced with, "Why is this happening to me?" We draw to every potion and herb we can find. We get into every prayer line to see if we can get this thing off of us. We have been prayed over for so long that the only thing we have left is our unswerving faith and dependability in Jesus.

The next time someone ask you why this "bad" thing occurred in their life; pass this book on to them. My hopes are that they will get a glimpse of their destiny and place in God. It is a joy to suffer for righteousness sake, but what happens when you do not feel it is for righteousness that you are going through? Bishop Mickie has exposed himself and becomes our modern day Job of suffering and is still doing the will of his Savior. He has taken his trials and tribulations and has transformed them to rejoicing moments of victory. Due to his trials, he has learned to think big and to stretch his imagination and faith as to what the Lord has called him to do.

I pray as you read this book, that you become infected with the same love and passion Dr. Mickie has learned in his life. Let his words minister to you, and be willing to say, "Broken, but not forsaken!" Yes, you may be in a travailing situation, but this book will help you receive your deliverance and victory.

Dr. Mickie you have enlightened us and opened unto us your life of suffering and your joys of triumph. I pray your revelation of grief and suffering will illuminate those who read this book with hope. I am confident it will be a tool everyone that has experienced or will experience calamities will use to help them overcome their situation and trust God. While we are going through the valley we must never forget a mountain is on the horizon—broken, but not forsaken!

Vincent C. Allen
Senior Pastor
Agape Fellowship Ministries, Inc.
Stafford, VA

PREFACE

Having traveled extensively around the world, I have had the opportunity to see many people existing in a state of brokenness. Their lives have been violently torn apart by spiritual attacks, physical disease, or they are emotionally rent into pieces. Coming from all walks of life, they portray a cool, calm, and collected demeanor when in actuality, they are hurting and ill equipped to cope with life itself. Pretending to be okay and in control, they eventually become casualties of their own visions. Under the weight of lost dreams, emotional scars, hurts, and physical maladies, Satan attempts to hand them a plan contrary to God's plan for their lives. .

It is the desire of the enemy for us to erroneously perceive our condition. If he can get us to believe our brokenness is for our demise then we will abort the ministries, plan, and visions that God has placed in each and everyone of us.

Because I have seen the destruction of ministries, businesses, relationships, and dreams, I felt compelled to pen these words of instructions, direction, encouragement and hope. Every effort has been made to reach persons who are broken in various areas of their lives. For those who are confounded by what is happening to them, may these words provide an explanation. For those experiencing dreams deferred, I have written these words to awaken urgency and expectancy for God's plan. I have written these words to impart inspiration and courage to those battling sickness and disease. I penned these words with the purpose of unlocking the faith, ambition, God-ordained self-image, and dreams that the Devil has held captive with the intention of subverting the will of God for us.

This book is by no means an exhaustive authority, but it is a vital link to the hidden thoughts of our hearts unearthed through these writings. The goal of this book is to underscore the reality that each one us has some type of problem or brokenness and unless we understand and face it, we stand to lose our overall purpose for existing. Finally, this book is strategically developed to show the reader where they are, instruct them in where they should be, and provoke them into getting there. Let this book bless your spirit, soul and body.

I earnestly pray that as you embark upon this journey, that the pages therein will richly enhance your thinking and that you will ascend to another measure of grace, mercy and prosperity on your way toward your divine destiny.

Dr. Jerlette Mickie

Author

CHAPTER ONE
BROKEN

*T*here is a time in the life of every child of God when they will enter into a season of brokenness. We do not expect it, ask for it, or desire it, yet this season is unavoidable. The inevitability of this period is not widely proclaimed in Christendom, nor is it a very popular subject. This season, however, demands our attention and must not be ignored.

> *To every thing there is a season, and a time to every purpose under the heaven (Ecclesiastes 3:1)*

It is during this time that God will permit life's circumstances to seemingly unravel right before our eyes. Sickness, disease, spiritual attacks, and financial disaster often announce our arrival into this very pivotal point in our lives.

To further compound matters, it is in this season when very often it is difficult to perceive the very presence of the Father. Our brokenness will often obscure God from our view and it is hard to perceive his Hand. It is imperative that we not allow our brokenness to nurture bitterness and anger towards God and others; otherwise we stand to miss the purpose for which God has allowed us to come into this season.

I must reiterate an earlier point that the inevitability of brokenness and suffering in the life of the child of God is not a popular or widely accepted subject. Christian bookstores cannot keep enough books in stock when they cover subjects such as the anointing, the blessings of the Lord, and spiritual warfare. However, Christians at large are often uninterested in teachings on suffering and how to enact Godly wisdom when in the middle of it.

Contrary to the lie that the enemy of our souls will try to purport, the season of brokenness was never meant for your demise. As a matter of fact, it is God's intention that your brokenness produces greater strength and tenacity in your life.

My brethren, count it all joy when ye fall into divers temptations;

Knowing this, that the trying of your faith worketh patience.

But let patience have her perfect work, that ye may be perfect and entire, wanting nothing. (James 1:2-4)

Once again I want to underscore the certainty of suffering in the life of every believer. Paul states that it is an absolute reality that the believer will encounter various trials and tests. Very often we are caught off-guard by the sudden attack or circumstances to which we find ourselves attached. Scripture, however, encourages us to consider these items as part of the process of life and not to be surprised by them.

God is not a sadistic tyrant who derives pleasure from seeing His children suffer. He has no desire to see His children without the things that He so wants to give them. He wants to see each one of us walking in total deliverance, prosperity, health, and functional relationships. Because He is omniscient, He knows that in order for us to possess those things and not abuse them, we must be mature enough to receive them.

Suffering through trials and tribulations is the tool that God uses to cultivate maturity and strength in us. Champions are made through the things they are willing to suffer. Although we wish we could redirect this, God recognizes that intrinsic in our response to our brokenness are the ingredients for our development.

Scripture admonishes us that trials of faith worketh (or lead to) patience. Patience can be defined as tried endurance, proven integrity, or maturity.

It should be noted that God does not arbitrarily allow us to go through trials just for the sake of seeing us broken. Parents do not enjoy seeing their children suffer, nor do they enjoy withholding things from them that they enjoy. On an emotional level, parents want to shield their children from all pain. They would cry all of their children's tears if possible simply because they love them. Unfortunately, life is not structured in a way where someone else can develop patience, endurance, and tenacity for us. A responsible parent will allow their children to experience discomfort, pain, or even heartache when it is aimed at developing greater character in them.

I am not seeking to expose why suffering produces character, because I believe that it is absolutely a work of the Grace of God that allows chaos to propel us into our divine destiny. That is the privilege that we have as children of God. No matter what we go through or how broken we may feel, it will absolutely work out in our favor.

And we know that all things work together for good to them that love God, to them who are the called according to his purpose. (Romans 8:28)

Many of you as you read this may say, "You don't understand. I just lost my job. I have just been diagnosed with cancer. My marriage is in disarray." But I say that as a son or daughter of God you have His Word that no matter what the situation, it will work together for your good. It may look absolutely bleak, but in the end God will reveal Himself in your circumstances.

One of the things that I've learned over the years is that it is far easier for us to believe God for others than for ourselves. It is easier for us to help others understand their suffering and pain than it is for us to understand our own. We stand ready to give profound information and insight. We fervently pray that God will sustain them through their season of adversity. We tell them that everything will work out okay and that God has His hand on their lives. We are even willing to rebuke the hand of the enemy off of our brothers and sisters in Christ will full faith that we indeed will have what we say.

Then your turn comes around.

What was so obvious and conspicuous to you when it was relative to your brother or sister's struggle becomes absolutely invisible when it is your turn to go through your season of brokenness. Finding the Word of the Lord to encourage yourself when your storm comes is a difficult and daunting task.

Why is it so easy for us to see the answer for others and not ourselves? Let us not put added precious on our hearts in finding this out. The scripture clearly declares:

Yea, and all that live godly in Christ Jesus shall suffer persecution. (2 Timothy 3:12)

Unfortunately, many of us fail to include ourselves in the "all that live godly" portion of the aforementioned scripture.

During the early years of my evangelistic career, I have probably laid hands on thousands of people. I have prayed for their deliverance from bondage, their loved ones to be released from prison, marriages to be restored, and the favor of God upon their finances. I have visited homes where drugs and alcohol have decimated the very fabric of the family. I have witnessed domestic violence in the home unable to fathom how humans can be so cruel to each other. Equipped with the Word of the Lord, however, I was able to go into those situations and watch God change the very atmosphere. Sometimes just a prayer spoken over a dying marriage or family situation can cause life to spring forth anew.

What is most interesting for me to recall about these times is that very often I was experiencing the some of the same things in my immediate circumstances. Sometimes, we as clergy can become so overwhelmed with the issues of others that we neglect our very own. We forget that the same God who sent us with the Word of the Lord for our brother, sister, or congregation, has a word for our situation as well.

I believe this situation can be expanded the whole of Christendom as well. It is often easy for us to encourage others in their time of crisis and believe God on behalf of others, yet we come up wanting relative to our own circumstances.

At these points, it is imperative to remember that God is Lord over your circumstances, the same way that we encouraged our brother or sister that He was Lord over theirs.

Guarding Our Perception

For as he thinketh in his heart, so is he...(Proverbs 23:7a)

When we are going through our periods of testing, it is important for us to remember to guard our perception. Very often, perception dictates reality. In other words, a situation may be one way, but the way we perceive it has a multiplicity of implications towards the outcome.

I remember while in military service, we were taken to the swimming pool area for our first qualification. Other than me, everyone appeared to be very excited. The guys were dressing out in their swim trunks eagerly awaiting a chance to show off their aquatic skills. I, on the other hand, pretended to have misplaced my swim trunks and if I had my way, they wouldn't show up until boot camp was over. I was trying to hide the fact that I could not swim. Not only could I not swim, but I was terrified of the water.

Per our instructor's orders, we were divided into two groups: swimmers and non-swimmers. For a brief moment, I thought that God had heard my silent cries for help and was allowing the cup of this trial to pass from me. The instructor ordered all of the swimmers to jump into the pool and swim the length of it. The swimmers executed his orders with patented efficiency.

For a moment, I lost myself in watching their excellence in swimming. I was forcefully brought out of my thoughts; however, when the instructor turned to the non-swimmers and began saying repeatedly, JUMP. I was stupefied. I was in stunned disbelief. My heart felt as if it were around my neck. My stomach had fallen to my knees, and they were shaking as if I were in a dance contest. I could hear myself crying out that I could not swim and that I did not want to die. I stood there absolutely paralyzed by fear.

Because none of the non-swimmers were eager to jump into the water, the instructor began to push us into the water, one by one. To this date I still recall my last word prior to him pushing me into the water: MOM! Unfortunately, as he pushed me into the water, he also came along for the ride thanks to Mickie Travels. Yes, I had inadvertently pulled the instructor into the water with me!

When I hit the water, I quickly sank to the bottom. My instinct kicked immediately and I began fighting to the top for air. As I barely pulled my head over the water, I took in as much air as possible screaming for help in between gulps. Although my eyes were closed, I could hear the water overtaking me again as I thrashed about struggling to keep from sinking. I could hear one of another instructor directing me to reach for one of the life vests, but instead of a life vest, I pulled yet another instructor into the pool with me. In those few moments, I knew for sure that my life was quickly coming to an end and thought that it was quite unfortunate for me to be dying at such a young age.

When all else had failed, one of the instructors commanded quite simply, "Open your eyes". When I finally arrested my emotions enough to obey his command, I realized that all of this time I had been standing in 4 feet of water. I stand 6ft 7inches tall. Along with the will to survive, the answer to my rescue simply rested in my adjusting my perception.

Until I opened my eyes (perception), I was drowning, confused, afraid, and headed toward imminent death. Once I opened my eyes, however, I realized that my circumstances did not possess the potency to kill me.

The same is true with respect to our trials, tribulations, and attacks from the enemy.

And Elisha prayed, and said, LORD, I pray thee, open his eyes, that he may. see. (2 Kings 6:17a)

When we are under attack, or our trial seems to be more than we can bear, the difference between defeat and total victory can be to simply open our eyes. Adjusting our perception to God's view will allow you to see the expected end that He has for you. It robs the enemy of his ability to deceive you into thinking that you will die from this sickness, that your marriage will fail, that you will always be broke, or that Satan's power is a superior force in your life. The difference between my walking out of the pool and drowning in 4 feet of water rested in my ability to right my perception of my circumstances. God's Word should always be the standard for our perceptions. If He says it, then that is what it is, no matter what it looks like.

In order to successful matriculate through your season of brokenness, you must first understand that it is a SEASON, and like all seasons, there is a time for it to end. Don't allow the enemy to manipulate your perception and have you move out of turn and thus delay your time of refreshing. Turn to the Word of God to accurately perceive what God is saying to you in your season of testing and how He wants you to respond.

CHAPTER TWO
GOD HAS A DIVINE PURPOSE FOR YOU

Before I formed thee in the belly I knew thee; and before thou camest forth out of the womb I sanctified thee, and I ordained thee a prophet unto the nations. (Jeremiah 1:5)

*J*ust as God spoke to Jeremiah the prophet, He wants us to understand that He recognizes us. He is familiar with us. We have no idea of who we really are sometimes. We may believe that we have a full understanding of who we are, but very often we do not.

Why? Because too often we attach ourselves to the ideas that we've set up about ourselves, or we adhere to what others have laid out as their perception of who we really are. We drag ourselves through our demanding and busy lives, satisfied with being what we consider productive and in tandem with our purpose, but missing out on the very purpose for our existence. We live our lives without meaning and true existence not ever really tapping into our true talents and capabilities.

We may feel that God has something for us, but we are not sure what it is or how to receive it. There is a deep sensing in many of us that there has got to be something more to this life than getting up, going to a job that you sort of like, going to church, and coming home. Because we are creatures of habit, however, it is easy for us to remain fixed in this non-existence/non-reality rather than connect with the abundant life that we have in Christ Jesus.

It is high time to awaken ourselves to who we are in God. We are sons and daughters of the God of the Universe! The God of Abraham, our forefathers.

And because ye are sons, God hath sent forth the Spirit of his Son into your hearts, crying, Abba, Father.

Wherefore thou are no more a servant, but a son; and if a son, then an heir of God through Christ. (Galatians 4:6-7)

Indeed we are heirs of salvation and joint-heirs with Christ. We are eternally connected to God in relationship that cannot be altered. He is our Father and we are His children.

It is the job of the enemy to distort our self-image so that we never really come into an understanding of who we are in Christ. If he can get us into error about our identity, he can rob us of our rights as children of God and keep us in bondage.

When we are broken and being tested it is easy to forget who you are because often the battle itself it attempting to redefine you in an unhealthy way.

GOD HAS A DIVINE PURPOSE FOR YOU

This is true even in church leadership. We have lost ourselves. We come to think of ourselves in terms of what we do and what ministry we serve on as a basis for our identity and worth.

For illustrative purposes, let's consider Sister Brown. Sister Brown has been leading the Praise Team of Revelation Church (fictional) for four years as one of their anointed praise and worship leaders. For reasons unknown to her, the pastor asks another sister on the team to assist in praise and worship diminishing Sister Brown's role somewhat. Sister Brown is beside herself. What is the pastor thinking? Not only is she anointed for praise and worship, but countless people tell her Sunday after Sunday that they come to church specifically to hear her lead them in worship because she is such a blessing.

Sister Brown is further baffled when the pastor asks her to assist with ushering temporarily. Church suddenly begins to lose its luster and appeal for her and she begins coming less and less until she eventually leaves Revelation Church and joins another ministry... where she can be used of God.

Had Sister Brown been looking at things through eyes of faith, she would have seen something different. God had not only designed her to be a praise and worship leader, but He destined her to become Pastor of Praise and Worship for Revelation Church. The seemingly diminished role wasn't designed to humiliate or demean her, but rather it was to be the tool with which he would show her pastor her worship not only in song, but also in service. This was to ultimately prick the pastor's heart to release her into her next level of anointing in the area of praise and worship.

Although I used this illustration is fictional, it presents some very real issues that we must understand. Too often we buy into only a small portion of who and what God has designed us to be. We get so comfortable where we are that it is difficult for God to promote us

11

BROKEN

to the next level. We must level our focus on who God has designed us to be and always be willing to embrace the next level of that state of being.

"Broken But Still on Assignment"

Being broken or in the middle of a test does not absolve of us the assignment that God has for us. As a matter of fact, brokenness may very well be a part of that assignment. It is time to get off the seat of pity, fear and disappointment. Wash the residue of sorrow and hurt from your heart and mind. Tell yourself that you shall live and not die and declare the works of the Lord (Psalm 118:17).

Whatever the test, it should not deter you from the assignment that God has laid out for you. He does not change His mind about what He has called you to do. Often, in spite of what you are feeling, you simply have to continue to do the work of the Lord. You have to continue reading the Word. You have to continue encouraging others, even when you yourself are discouraged.

And he said unto me, Son of man, can these bones live? And I answered, O Lord God, thou knowest. (Ezekiel 37:3)

In this chapter of scripture, God had given Ezekiel an assignment to prophesy to dry bones in a valley. When He asked Ezekiel if the bones could live, Ezekiel answered honestly. He did not know.

Very often God will have you on assignment and you have absolutely no idea how things are going to work out. We must understand that our knowledge of how things are going to work out is not precluding our assignment. Not knowing whether the bones would live or remain in the state they were already in, Ezekiel obediently prophesied to the valley of dry bones. It was then that God moved.

We must learn to faithfully perform that which God requires of us even while in our state of brokenness. You may not see how encouraging someone else that God is going to meet their financial need while you are wondering how yours will be met is beneficial to you. But could it be that while you are ministering to the needs of someone else, as God has assigned you, that He is making provision for you? Or maybe the very words of life that you need for situation won't come forth until you speak on behalf of God to someone else. I can't tell you how many times in ministry that I've been preaching and realized that the answer to some of my most stressful situations came forth out of my own mouth.

For ye have need of patience, that, after ye have done the will of God, ye might receive the promise. (Hebrews 10:36)

We are admonished in scripture to hang onto our confidence and persist in the assignment to which God has called us. We are encouraged that by doing so we are developing and nurturing patience and that a promise lies just beyond our faith.

Sometimes that means encouraging someone when you are discouraged yourself. It could mean blessing someone financially when you are in need of a financial blessing. Perhaps it means ministering grace to the broken heart of someone else when your heart is broken in a million pieces.

Remaining faithful to the task before you in the middle of trials bears fruit that pleases our Father and is a sign that broken pieces still work!

BROKENESS WILL GIVE DIRECTION

Of all of the points that I have made throughout this text, I have attempted to underscore this one more than the others. God does not allow us to go through brokenness without purpose. He is still in control of our lives and our destiny, no matter how chaotic things may appear to be.

Oftentimes, our pain blinds us from seeing God's presence in our lives. We feel abandoned and forsaken in this season. Of course there are some very spiritual persons out there who will tell you that you are not spiritual for feeling this way. To be quite honest, however, it is part of the human experience to not necessarily enjoy the experience of pain.

And he went a little farther, and fell on his face, and prayed, saying, O my Father, if it be possible, let this cup pass from me: nevertheless not as I will, but as thou wilt. (Matthew 26:39)

Jesus, the only begotten Son of the Father, in his humanity, wanted to resist the season of affliction that was soon to befall him. Jesus knew full well the physical pain and agony that was set before him. He understood the overwhelming pressure that the weight of the world's sin would be on his shoulders. More than anything else, he understood the agony of separation from the Father that he would feel as a result our sins being laid to his charge.

No matter how spiritual we try to pass ourselves off as, there are times when we sense that God is taking us through a season of brokenness and we simply do not want to submit to it. It does not take away from our sonship to acknowledge that we are human and don't enjoy suffering. The truth of the matter is if we could have it our way, there would be no suffering in our lives at all.

Jesus provides an excellent model of how our attitude should be postured toward of period of testing.

He went away again the second time, and prayed, saying, O my Father, if this cup may not pass away from me, except I drink it, thy will be done. (Matthew 26:42)

Although it is clear that in his humanity Jesus did not want to suffer through his trial of dying for the sins of the world, he conceded to the will of the Father because he understood the purpose of God for his life.

It is absolutely critical that we as believers understand the plan that God has for our lives.

And we know that all things work together for good to them that love God, to them who are the called according to his purpose. (Romans 8:28).

According to HIS purpose is the point that I want to stand out in your minds. Things work together for good to them who are called not according to their own purposes, but HIS purpose. When we began to understand the direction that God is taking our lives in, we can stand on that scripture and command that our circumstances, no matter how dark they are, work for good in our lives.

Jesus yielded to the will of the Father in light of the purpose God had for his life. The very purpose of his life on the earth was to redeem fallen man back to the Father. Understanding his purpose helped Jesus to endure an unpleasant season for the greater good. He understood that things were not in disarray, but that all things were still under the gubernatorial reign of the Father.

The steps of a good man are ordered by the Lord: and he delighteth in his way. Though he fall, he shall not be utterly cast down: for the Lord upholdeth him with his hand. (Psalm 37:23-24)

No matter how out of sorts' things may appear to be, God is clear on what He has destined for your life. He will not allow your circumstances to destroy you. He will not allow your situations to rob you of the purpose that He has placed within you.

Instead, He will cause you to rise in the midst of your circumstances. Those very things that seemed as if they were going to overwhelm you will become the biggest testaments to the grace of God on your life.

Tests Serve As Reminders of God's Divine Purpose

I mentioned earlier that it is imperative that we guard our perceptions as they very often dictate reality in our lives. This principle is resident in the idea that we are often reminded of God's purpose for our lives while in the middle of our brokenness.

For I reckon that the sufferings of this present time are not worthy to be compared with the glory which shall be revealed in us. (Romans 8:18)

At the time that the Apostle Paul was inspired to write this text, Christians were being persecuted for just believing in Jesus. He admonished the early Church that the suffering that they were experiencing was not in the same class as the glory that God had foreordained for their lives. The persecution they were experiencing was obscuring the overall plan of God from the minds of the early believers. Paul's motive was to encourage them to allow their persecution to point them toward the awesome promise that they had in God. He pointed them to their inheritance in the faith, which was incorruptible.

We must adhere to the same standard. It is tempting to get so caught up in our present circumstances that we forget the promises that God has made to us concerning our lives. We must allow our testing to remind us of our purpose and that God is perfecting those things that concern us.

Being confident of this very thing, that he which hath begun a good work in you will perform it until the day of Jesus Christ. (Phillipians 1:6)

It may seem that you are stuck in the middle of a season of brokenness, but God has not left you to fend for yourself. He will complete in you everything that He has started. We must believe this if we are to overcome. Allow this season of brokenness to point you back to what God has promised you. There are some promises that God has made to you many years ago that you are yet waiting on their manifestation. Instead of becoming depressed and buying into the lie that none of your dreams will come true, allow your tests to remind you that God's truth endures to all generations. If God has purposed it, it shall stand.

Quitting Is Too Expensive

Now that we understand that brokenness is often the road to our divine destiny, it becomes apparent that quitting is too expensive.

For our light affliction, which is but for a moment, worketh for us a far more exceeding and eternal weight of glory; (2 Corinthians 4:17)

We've already established that suffering, by the divine work of grace, produces character in the life of the believer. When en route to your divine destiny, quitting cannot be apart of your internal thought process. Yes, there is pain, heartache, fatigue, and every other thing that comes with suffering, but we must not lose heart. The very act of not quitting develops patience in our constitution.

Cast not away therefore your confidence, which hath great recompense of reward. For ye have need of patience, that, after ye have done the will of God, ye might receive the promise. (Hebrews 10:35-36)

There are two things that I want to underscore from the above text. We are first admonished by this scripture not to quit because our confidence will pay off in a great reward. What is that great reward? It is our destiny coming to fruition. It is the promises of God concerning our circumstances coming to pass. It is the hand of the enemy rebuked off of our finances. It is healing for our physical bodies and health to our souls. So, in light of all of this you can understand why we are admonished not to give up.

The Devil knows full well that he cannot rob us of our destiny. He does not possess that kind of power. No matter how largely he presents himself, he has no authority over the destiny that God has placed in us nor can he directly influence the outcome of our trials. The only thing he can do is deceive is to the point where we walk away from our purpose. If he can get us to buy into his lies that God will not come through on our behalf or to become embittered by our circumstances, then we forfeit our right to receive our inheritance, deliverance, healing, financial blessings, and every other blessing God has designated for our lives.

The second portion of the scripture outlines our need for patience and the inevitability of receiving God's blessing after we have obeyed. Too often, we desire the promises of God without obeying His orders.

Unfortunately, it does not work that way. Very often, God will require some things of us that we will only see the blessing inherent in them after we have obeyed his directive.

The life of Jesus illustrates this point exactly:

And being found in fashion as a man, he humbled himself, and became obedient unto death, even the death of the cross. (Phillipians 2:8)

Scripture directs us to look to Jesus as our example of how not to quit.

Wherefore seeing we also are compassed about with so great a cloud of witnesses, let us lay aside every weight and the sin which doth so easily beset us, and let us run with patience the race that is set before us,

Looking unto Jesus the author and finisher of our faith; who for the joy that was set before him endured the cross, despising the shame, and is set down at the right hand of the throne of God. (Hebrews 12: 1-2)

If we are to look to Jesus as an example to complete our course, we must understand the method by which he fulfilled the will of God by holding fast through his time of testing.

Jesus Acknowledged His Emotions:

There is a common misconception in Christendom today that Christians do not experience fear, anxiety, frustration, anger, or any of the other emotions that are a part of the human experience. Our understanding of what it means to be spiritual does not leave much room for us to be human. In effect, we go from one extreme to the other. We are either really standing in faith rebuking doubt, fear, anxiety, and any other weapon the enemy might use against. Or, at the opposite extreme, we are standing in complete defeat, totally mastered by our emotions.

God is a God of design and balance. To the average Christian, one cannot be standing in faith, but experience fear and or anxiety. Scripture, however, does not bear that out. When we look at the life of Jesus Christ we see that he experienced a vast array of emotions while going through his time of testing. This is particularly true in the Garden of Gethsemane.

Then said he unto them, My soul is exceeding sorrowful, even unto death: tarry ye here and watch with me. (Matthew 26:38)

Dear brother, dear sister, make no mistake about it, there will come a time when you can be under attack so heavy or tested so strictly, that your emotions will become involved. We as Christians must learn to acknowledge our emotions without being subject to them. It is the way that we acknowledge our emotions that makes the difference. Notice that Jesus directed his emotional outlet to the Father. It is not disrespectful or unspiritual to communicate honestly with the Father about how you are feeling about what you are going through. For the parent who loses a child, it is not unspiritual to express to God your grief, confusion, anger, and utter hopelessness. Like Jesus, however, just remember to direct your emotional outlet to the Father. For the person with bills due immediately and no finances to pay them, it is no offense to the Father to express that you are concerned about how your needs will be met.

It is absurd to think that you are not living up to God's standard by repressing emotions that he already knows you are experiencing. There is nothing that you can hide from Him. He is aware of your thoughts, feelings, and emotions. So trust Him enough to vent your feelings to Him.

Once we've directed our emotional outlet to the Father, we must be careful to use His Word and His directives as our standard for action.

Now is my soul troubled; and what shall I say? Father, save me from this hour: but for this cause came I unto this hour. (John 12: 27)

Although emotionally Jesus was feeling the pressure of his road to the cross, he was yet able to conform to the will of the Father. He subordinated His emotions to the will and directives of the Father.

O my Father, if this cup may not pass away from me, except I drink it, thy will be done. (Matthew 26: 42b)

Perhaps the most challenging part of following Jesus' example is after we've vented our emotions, we must align them with the Word of God and what God has directed us to do. If we do not do this, we stand to be ruled by every emotional whim that comes.

Your rent is due and you don't have the funds to make payment. You've vented your concern to the Father and expressed your need to Him. The only thing left to do now is remind Him of His promise to keep you. Stand on His Word in faith and wait for Him to make a way. At that point, the only responsibility you have is stand on his Word and hold fast to your profession of faith.

Look to the Promise for Inspiration

As I have explained earlier, it is far easier for us to tell someone to hold on during his or her time of testing than it is for us to actually do it ourselves. There are times when you are so downtrodden by our trials that it seems impossible to hold our heads up. It is imperative for us to remember that it is at those times that we must look to what God has promised us as our source of inspiration.

The Word says Jesus endured suffering for the joy that was set before him. In other words, he was able to look with eyes of faith to the time when he would be restored to his place of fellowship with the Father in all of his former glory. He understood that his purpose for coming into the world was to reconcile God and man and utterly defeat the authority of sin in the earth. Standing between Jesus and completion of his assignment was the cross and the unfathomable suffering that he was enduring. Jesus was able to look beyond the initial pain and discomfort of his current situation to a time when his glory would be restored.

Many times the only thing standing between us and our destiny is the temporary suffering or trial that we are enduring. It is in those moments that we must look to those promises that God has made to us with eyes of faith for inspiration to hold on until our victory manifests itself in our circumstances.

Paul admonishes us to look beyond our circumstances to our legacy in Christ for inspiration:

For which cause we faint not; but though our outward man perish, yet the inward man is renewed day by day.

For our light affliction, which is but for a moment, worketh for us a far more exceeding and eternal weight of glory;

While we look not at the things which are seen, but at the things which are not seen: for the things which are seen are temporal; but the things which are not seen are eternal. (II Corinthians 4: 16-18)

If we are to make it successfully through our season of brokenness, we must learn to look beyond our present suffering to the promises that God has laid before us. Does that mean that you ignore the pain that you are in? Certainly not. I have stated earlier that it is part of the human experience to experience pain and to be affected by it. We must, however, like Jesus learn to look beyond our present circumstances to the promises of God that are set before us.

It is easier to look to the promise when we recognize that are season of suffering is temporary. Paul said that our affliction, which is temporary, produces for us an eternal weight of glory. In other words, the pain that we experience now won't compare to the promise we inherit in Christ if we hold our faith firm to the end.

For I reckon that the sufferings of this present time are not worthy to be compared with the glory which shall be revealed in us. (Romans 8:18)

Things operate paradoxically in the Kingdom of God. In God's kingdom, suffering, brokenness, and tribulation are the paths to glory. We must arm ourselves with this knowledge and use it to encourage our hearts while in our season of testing.

CHAPTER THREE
OPERATING WITH
THE HURT PIECES

When God carries out His purposed plan, it is often through the hands of hurting people. Those who have gone through rough circumstances and experiences. People who have seemingly been handed the short end of the stick of life. Those who aren't even expecting to make it in life. Those who have been grappling with the crumbs of society just hoping for enough to keep it together.

Those kinds of odds laid against us by the enemy give God the perfect opportunity to manifest His glory and sovereignty. One word from God can change the entire situation. One word from God can bring order to all of the chaos. One word from God can dry up cancer in your body.

We must lay hold of the fact that if God is allowing us to go through suffering, then He has a plan in mind for us and that He will bring us to our expected end.

The word which came to Jeremiah from the LORD, saying,

Arise and go down to the potter's house, and there I will cause thee to hear my words. (Jeremiah1: 7)

Then I went down to the potter's house, and, behold, he wrought a work on the wheels.

And the vessel that he made of clay was marred in the hand of the potter: so he made it again another vessel, as seemed good to the potter to make it.

Then the word of the LORD came to me, saying,

O house of Israel, cannot I do with you as this potter? saith the LORD, Behold, as the clay is in the potter's hand, so are ye in mine hand, O house of Israel. (Jeremiah 18:1-6)

Regardless of what you are feeling, God is pioneering things in your life with purpose in mind. While you are in the furnace of affliction, He is refining your vessel and removing the impurities contained therein. He is allowing your circumstances to shape you into a better person.

Why is it then that although we know these things, we remain blind to them while in the middle of suffering? I believe it is because we fail to renew our minds to God's Word. As a matter of fact, we tend to renew our minds to the things that people are saying about our situation rather than God. This can be very dangerous as we can begin to view ourselves the way that others have defined us by their words.

Broken Mentally

I can recall a period of my life that I can only describe as hellish. As a young boy, the adults told me in my life that I was useless. I was told that I would not be anything in life and that I would be just like my biological father, who was described to me as a shiftless deadbeat. I was branded a nobody, without any value, dreams, vision, or anything else to hold on to.

Having laid eyes on my natural father only two times, everything they said about him seemed to be true. Because what was said about my natural father appeared to be true, it was easy for me to begin to accept this horrible image of myself. There was no way to defend myself from these words as any response contrary to them incited physical repercussions that my young body could not handle.

We use to say in those days that sticks and stones would break our bones, but words would never hurt us. That couldn't be further from the truth. Words spoken to me in my youth absolutely devastated me. Those negative words shaped my worldview and perception of myself.

For it was not an enemy that reproached me; then could I have borne it: neither was it he that hated me that did magnify himself against me; then I would have hid myself from him:

But it was thou, a man mine equal, my guide, and mine acquaintance. (Psalm 55: 12-13)

In the previously referenced scripture, David is crying out to God to comfort his heart after being betrayed by a friend. Words from strangers or people without relevance do not have the same impact as those from a loved one. Consider a stranger walking up to you on the street and telling you that you are no good and a worthless bum.

You might initially recoil at those words, but ultimately you would put them in proper context as that person knows nothing about you and you know even less about them.

It is not as easy to do this with loved ones, however. We are vulnerable to them. When we are young, we are dependent upon them for food, clothing, emotional support, and shelter. We rely on our loved ones to reinforce our feelings that we are loved and that the world is a safe and secure place. When this relationship is abused, the results can be exponential.

Very often, the words that devastate us and by which we derive our self-image are not from those that we would consider our adversaries. Unfortunately, these words often come from the lips of mothers, fathers, siblings, or even people that we consider to be close friends.

I had been attending church since I was 6 years old, but as a young man enduring all of the mental abuse I was experiencing, I did not know how God viewed me or what He said about my condition. Unfortunately, like so many today, I was attending church consistently, but had no real relationship with God.

Perhaps the most dangerous component of my youthful scenario other than my lack of relationship with God is that I allowed myself to be defined by the words of others rather than the Word of God.

CHAPTER FOUR
BROKENNESS PRESENTS AN OPPORTUNITY TO RESPOND TO GOD'S WORD

For as the rain cometh down, and the snow from heaven, and returneth not thither, but watereth the earth, and maketh it bring forth and bud, that it may give seed to the sower, and bread to the eater:

So shall my word be that goeth forth out of my mouth: it shall not return unto me void, but it shall accomplish that which I please, and it shall prosper in the thing whereto I sent it. (Isaiah 55:10-11)

As sons and daughters of God we must absolutely rest assured that God's Word is the final authority on our situation. According to scripture, God's Word is not impotent, therefore if He has declared that something shall be, it will absolutely come to fruition. God's

Word is His seed. When God plants His Word into something, a harvest is inevitable.

Our response to God's Word should be concurrence. Our situations present an opportunity for us to respond to God's Word either in the affirmative or the negative. If our response is in agreement with our situation as opposed to God's Word, we will have the fruit of our response. The power lies in what we respond to.

Key to realizing change in our lives is for us to begin to agree with what God says about us and our situation.

And be not conformed to this world: but be ye transformed by the renewing of your mind, that ye may prove what is that good, and acceptable, and perfect, will of God. (Romans 12:2)

To renew is to "make new again". Renewing our minds to God's Word means that we exchange our ideas about a given situation for God's idea concerning the situation. It means that we renovate our paradigm from all of the negative thoughts that were planted by family members and those who were close to us to what God's Word says about our circumstances.

As a young man that had experienced mental and emotional abuse, my self-image was absolutely distorted. Because I was told that everything that I put my hands to would fail, I begin to believe it. I didn't believe that I would ever be able to escape the terror of my childhood or live up to the unrealistic and impossible standards that were set for me just to be accepted by those who were charged with caring for me.

I thank God daily for the potency of His Word. I don't care what you're going through or what you're experiencing; if God can get His Word in you it will change the entire situation.

BROKENNESS PRESENTS AN OPPORTUNITY TO RESPOND TO GOD'S WORD

Though I was mentally abused throughout my childhood, I was never restricted from going to church. It was in church that I began to hear through God's Word that I was more than what people were telling me that I was. As I grew older, God began to reveal Himself to me in His Word and I went from just knowing about Him to actually knowing and experiencing Him in relationship.

I saw in the Word of God that I was fearfully and wonderfully made, and that although my natural father may have been all those things that I was told, I did not have to become those things. I saw that God wanted me to be successful in everything that I did. I saw that He had a plan and a purpose for my life and I began to immerse myself in getting to know Him.

This did not happen overnight. I had been verbally and emotionally abused for years and it would take some time for me to get the mental breakthrough that was required for me to go to the next level. I had to intentionally meditate on God's Word concerning my life to undue all of the negative thoughts and emotions that the devil had me in bondage to as a result of my abuse.

I first had to agree that God's Word was the final authority concerning my life and then renew my negative thoughts and the words of others to God's Word concerning my life. Note that I had to actively apply God's Word to my situation using my mouth to declare life to my situation. I had to speak life to myself for myself; not for others but for me.

Renewal of the mind is not for the slothful or faint of heart. The mind is an awesome mechanism. It contains our will, emotions, intellect, and overall thought processes. There are tons of books written on the mind aimed at helping us to better understand it. It is where we store all of the information that we receive. It is the context against which we view the world. If one's mind is tainted, then it is fairly reasonable to conclude that their overall worldview and outlook on life is also tainted.

Words are the vehicles by which access is granted to the mind. As children when we were told to remember something what is the first thing that we began to do? We repeated whatever we were trying to remember over and over again until it was securely imprinted in our minds. How do you get children to remember ABCs? How do you remember a telephone number? Repetition. Now consider the impact of negative words repeated to someone during the course of their childhood or even as an adult.

Death and life are in the power of the tongue: and they that love it shall eat the fruit thereof. (Proverbs 18:21)

If we are to ever rid ourselves of the negative images and perceptions that we've allowed the devil and other people to set up in our lives, we must speak life to our situations.

This is where the connection between faith and works is underscored. James said that faith without works is dead (James 2:17). We must actively train our minds how we desire for it to think. We must actively meditate on the Word of God to feed the Mind of Christ that lies within us so that we are thinking in accord with the will of God for our lives and our situation.

It takes action and effort to replace negative thought patterns with God's Word. Think it about for one moment. Psychologists tell us that by the time a child reaches 14 years old, he or she essentially has in place the basic thought constructs from which they will operate for the duration of their lives. In other words our mental framework is securely in place fairly early in our lives. Whether or not that mental framework is positive or negative depends largely upon what it is fed.

BROKENNESS PRESENTS AN OPPORTUNITY TO RESPOND TO GOD'S WORD

As I mentioned previously, words, good or bad, feed the mind and nurture it. The propensity or inclination toward things positive or negative is predicated upon what has been nurturing it.

When this is taken into account, it is easy to see why spoken words have such a profound effect upon us. Consider the young girl who is told by an insensitive adult in their life that they are destined to be a failure. Imagine the young boy who is told that all men in his family are no good and he will grow up to be no good just like all the other men in his family line. Those words take root in the growing mindset of that young child and begin to manifest themselves in the child's actions, perceptions, and overall mentality.

Without Godly intervention, it is fairly logical to conclude that negative words and their adverse effects don't diminish with time. Instead they breed low self-esteem, which can manifest itself in substance abuse, promiscuity, and inappropriate relationships, among a host of other issues.

We as Christians are quick to judge and condemn a person who may be manifesting symptoms of a problem that is much deeper than what we see. The young girl who is promiscuous is not just "fast". Perhaps she is looking for words of approval, encouragement, and validation. Consider the possibility that she may be wrestling with words spoken over her as a child telling her that no one would ever love her and believes that offering herself physically is the only way to merit love.

The young man who appears angry at the world may very well be grappling with the verbal and/or physical abuse that he suffered through as a child. Perhaps he is "angry" because he was unable to prevent or change his situation at so young of an age.

Thank God that neither Satan nor man has the final say so when it comes to our destiny! We still have the opportunity to reverse what the enemy has set in motion for our lives. God can take all of the bad things that have happened to us and turn them around for our good. I don't care how intense the abuse was and what type it was, God is able to reverse what the enemy has put in place for you.

God has placed the potency of His strength at our disposal by way of His Word. We activate His power to tear down the mental strongholds the enemy has set up in our minds by declaring His Word. The Word applied to any area of brokenness will bring forth healing and life.

It is the spirit that quickeneth; the flesh profiteth nothing: the words that I speak unto you, they are spirit, and they are life. (John 6:63)

We must train our mind to think in line with God's Word. The Bible says that the carnal mind or the mind that is not renewed to God's way of thinking is hostile or in opposition with God (Romans 8:7).

We must command our thoughts to line up with God's way of thinking with the full understanding that we are going to come up against a lot of things that we previously held as absolute. As a young boy, I discovered in God's Word that I was fearfully and wonderfully made. This was completely contrary to everything that I had heard growing up. People were telling me that I was going to be a no good alcoholic just like my biological father. In direct contrast, my Heavenly Father told me in His Word that His plan for me was one of success, not evil, and that He had a positive destination for my life (Jeremiah 29:11).

Things did not change for me, however, until I went beyond merely knowing what God's Word said about me and my situation to confessing and declaring His Word over my situation. It was then that I begin to develop a more intimate relationship with Him. It was

BROKENNESS PRESENTS AN OPPORTUNITY TO RESPOND TO GOD'S WORD

then that I began to challenge the things that were said about me and categorize them properly. It was when I professed the Word of God that I began to see the nature of God and His paternal dealings. The God that I discovered was loving and nurturing and had left me a rich inheritance in righteousness.

There is something intrinsic in the Word of God that tends to change your mindset when declared over your circumstances.

Blessed is the man that walketh not in the counsel of the ungodly, nor standeth in the way of sinners, nor sitteth in the seat of the scornful. (Psalm 1:1)

There are inherent blessings in not walking in the counsel of the ungodly. The opposite of walking in the counsel of the ungodly is walking in Godly counsel. What is Godly counsel? It is the counsel of the Word of God.

But his delight is in the law of the LORD; and in his law doth he meditate day and night. (Psalm 1:2)

The writer encourages us in the scripture to meditate, think on, and confess the Word of the Lord daily. Confessing God's Word over your circumstances should be a daily habit that you consistently employ. Meditating on the Word of the Lord imprints it on your heart and in your soul. Prior to meditating on the Word of God, your response to an adverse situation would be one of fear and negativity. After embracing the Word of God as a way of life, however, you will soon find that instead of fear, a Godly confidence and boldness will spring from your heart as you confront your adversity in faith.

And he shall be like a tree planted by the rivers of water, that bringeth forth his fruit in his season; his leaf also shall not wither; and whatsoever he doeth shall prosper. (Psalm 1:3)

We are told that the individual who meditates, thinks on, and confesses the Word of the Lord will be like a tree planted by the rivers of water. A tree planted by the water has roots that run deep. There is no shallowness in that tree. It is stable. It can endure the storms of life and remain in place.

It is easy to expand that to our Christian walk, particularly when we are going through our season of suffering. We are to be so rooted in the Word of God that come hell or high water, we remain stable and consistent. Feasting on the Word of God brings with it the stability to remain constant no matter what the situation because we are assured that what God has ordained will indeed come to fruition.

Not only will being rooted in the Word of God yield stability through the fiercest adversity and trials, but it will also provide protection and prosperity.

...his leaf also shall not wither; and whatsoever he doeth shall prosper. (Psalm 1:3b)

The Word of God will serve as a shield to protect us from things that the enemy would use to destroy us. If the enemy were to have his way, the trials that we face would kill us. Our Heavenly Father, however, provides protection from the tactics of the enemy. That protection is found in the counsel of His Word. God's Word assures us that no weapon that forms against us will prosper.

Moreover, when we are firmly rooted in God's Word, fully assured that it is the absolute authority, everything that we put our hands to will absolutely prosper. We can sow a seed and expect a harvest. We can declare our right to be healed according to the Word of God and expect for it to manifest. We can declare victory and deliverance in our lives and expect to see results.

CHAPTER FIVE
BROKEN PHYSICALLY & SPIRITUALLY

But he was wounded four our transgression, he was bruised for our iniquities: the chastisement of our peace was upon him; and with his stripes we are healed. (Isaiah 53:5)

As I right this chapter in it's entirety, I come to empty myself the more as I go back a few years where my life was just hanging in the balance.

As I take snapshots of my life from all angles to provide a personal example of how God still used my broken pieces and the pieces that remained in tact in my life, I have and always will thank my Lord and Savior Jesus Christ for touching my life in a physical way.

It was early in the month of February 1987 that while sitting in the doctor's office with my wife Leona, that I would receive news that would forever change my life. The results of the battery of tests that he had put me through didn't look good. His diagnosis was even worse. He told me that I had ALS, also known as Lou Gehrig's disease.

ALS stands for Amyotrophic Lateral Sclerosis and it is a fatal neuromuscular disease characterized by progressive muscle weakness resulting in paralysis.

My doctor went on to inform me that there was no known cure for ALS at the time, and that there was essentially a one in one million survival rate. In two years, he stated, your motor system will be completed affected; you'll be an invalid and unable to help yourself.

Never in my life I had I received more shocking news than what seemed to be coming out of the doctor's mouth. Everything seemed to be going in slow motion as I felt my body shrinking in response and my heart seemingly breaking into one million pieces. How could this be happening to me?

Leona and I held hands tightly as the doctor continued his grim report. Thank God for a praying wife, who always seems to discern my heart without my having to articulate what is going on inside. I could hear her whispering praises and petitions on my behalf as she caressed my hand and back.

I was instructed by my doctor to refrain from a lot of physical exercises and activities as they would likely escalate my condition and cause me to experience medical problems sooner than anticipated. This was going to be a problem. Anyone who knows me knows that I am a man of excitement and energy. I am a sports fanatic as well. Generally speaking, I am energetic and dynamic in just about everything that I do.

BROKEN PHYSICALLY & SPIRITUALLY

Now I am told to cease as much physical activity as possible and essentially wait to become paralyzed.

Hurt and disappointment seemed to be swallowing me whole in that office on that day in particular. I was in a major crisis. The doctor had just given me a pronouncement of death in a matter of two years. If I were to completely change my life and not do anything at all, perhaps I could squeeze another year or two out of it. It appeared that life was going to be a series of ups and downs for me with no real meaning. What about my life? What about my children, who I am so attached to? What about my wife of then, thirteen years? This could not be happening.

Although I was an emotional wreck, nothing came to the surface externally. I would not dare cry in front of my wife or the doctor, for that matter. Somewhere at that point, I decided that this was my problem alone.

Once again, I must thank my Father for my wife Leona. Leona stood by my side the entire way, even though sometimes I didn't know how to let her in. Often when we are faced with physical disease, we lash out in anger at the very ones who are providing assistance to us. We must gain our perspective, appreciating the ones that God is using to get us through our period of illness, and move forward with the vision.

God is not a man, that he should lie; neither the son of man, that he should repent: hath he said, and shall he not do it? Or hath he spoken, and shall he not make it good? (Numbers 23:19)

There are many of you, who like me, have been given a death sentence due to a physical ailment of some sort. It is difficult for you to accept it, however, because you still feel the ministry that God is birthing inside of you. You still feel the call of God to change lives and impart grace to those without. There is still destiny unfulfilled that must come to pass before you leave this life.

My brother, my sister, let me tell you something. God has not changed His mind concerning you and your destiny. If God has ordained that you complete a task, answer a call, or touch a life, then it shall be unto you according to your faith.

Declaring the end from the beginning, and from ancient times the things that are not yet done, saying, My counsel shall stand, and I will do all my pleasure. (Isaiah 46:10)

We must understand that God is never surprised by the things that happen to us. As a matter of fact, He knows everything that ever will happen to you in your entire life. So when God calls you to a particular task or ministry, He is aware of every temptation, frailty, and attack the enemy will place on your life. Yet He still calls you.

If that is the case, then the answer, once again, lies with whose report we choose to believe. We can either accept death, or we can choose life, according to the Word of God.

My choice was quite simple. I could choose to believe the report of the doctor, go home, take it easy for two years, and die. Or, I could hang on to the fact that there was still work in the earth for me to do. There was still destiny that was calling me into my future.

Thank God, I chose to believe the Report of the Lord. I absolutely refused to accept that I was going to shrivel up and die. Don't get me wrong, I knew that this was a serious condition and that I was going to have to fight with everything inside of me to stay on top. But I also knew that I had a ministry inside of me. I was on divine assignment to preach, teach, and empower and propel young men and women to excellence.

As I bring this chapter to a close, I want to share a prayer of hope with you to encourage your heart:

I ask you Father, the Giver of breath, life, and mercy to minister grace to the readers of this book. Oh Giver of hope and comfort, grant us peace and strength. Bestow upon us the virtue of patience to endure this time of testing and see it to its conclusion and manifestation of your will. Help us deal with every physical setback that comes to void out our purpose, arrest our hope, and destroy our dreams of being what you've destined us to be. Father help us turn our periods of procrastination and lack into forward motion toward our destiny. Help us to ward off every device that comes to impede our progress.

Father we ask that your hands of protection surround us as we again journey forward in the things you have prepared for us. This we pray in the matchless name of the Lord Jesus Christ. Amen. Now expect God to invade your circumstances!

BROKEN SPIRITUALLY

Things that happen in the world we live in are seldom herald as a surprise, but often expected for the times we are all living it. While this may be true to some point of view, the spiritual side of this equation would appear the total opposite if something was happening from the negative perspective. The truth is, even in spiritual matters nothing is becoming a surprise either; for some of the most unexpected fireworks will happen in ministry. Some of these fireworks that bring God no glory will bring you as a leader to your knees calling for God's wisdom to direct your faculties. There are so many things that can happen in the spare of the moment, to break down your spirit, your trust in God, trust in the vision he imparted to you. Have you ever had a dream, a vision, a desire, and a plan, a promise aborted before your eyes? What about the faith you put in others, swiftly departing you, base off of circumstance out of your control. How about something you felt God promise you a long time ago, and as of to date it hasn't happen yet.

The bitterness of ministry is the reality of facing a failure in what was once a promise. A sure thing, an absolute gone obsolete, a dream now just a memory, to you your life is becoming a book of pages uncompleted, torn by wrong perspectives, ill advised decisions, investing in the people of no vision. At one point we look all so prosperous and blessed, with a plan that would affect the world around you, giving yourself and those you are targeting hope. This is often too familiar of a cunning culprits work of an inside job. Your trust is being monitored, your advice is being questioned, your vision impaired, your hands have become unsteady, your speech has become blurred, It is so important to know what God has called you to do and pursue that, the ministry alone is a tedious adventure, there will be good and bad days, wet and dry weeks, fast and slow months, prosperous and not so prosperous years, we must keep our focus center to the saving of souls, or we will become as some often have, caught up in how what we did, how what we played, how what we spoke, how what we sang, how and what we gave. I come to learn through it all, the vision has to be so large that only God can work it, and so precise that mans intellect Is not able to alter it.

Society views our accomplishment, not in remembering what we did while living, but how well we did it, or how well we practice what we preached. I come to examine my season, that regardless, the nature of my circumstance, any time we attempt to operate or covenant ourselves with the handy work of God, there will always be some form of conspiracy to damage you, the leader and the people associate with your purpose to bring it in to reality. It is therefore important, that one must understand the defining line about purpose and destiny. If understand it and choose to continue, you will succeed while conquering the failures that once was your vision. Stay focus, so that if God really called you to work, he will have you to finish and it will be all the worthwhile no matter what has or will take place.

Finally so many people have left ministries, businesses and family members alike, trying to find the missing pieces of their life, that they couldn't find in others. There is no greater pain that can be so overwhelming and ongoing than the conflicts of doing ministry. I have come to understand that it doesn't take much to hurt in ministry; especially if it is your heart desire to help and bless people. People will often hurt you leaving no apologies and justification. It serves every leader to have their heart fixed with Jesus Agape love. You will have your days were you feel great and ready to challenge, provoke and conqueror the world, only to wake up with a reality check. Often times leaders in ministry will not hurt just for souls, but merely just for there needs to be met, spiritually, mentally and physically. In spite all the hype about the great men and women of the gospel, we hurt, we pain, we go through, we struggle, and we cry. Though I held it all back, I learned the way to deal with brokenness even as a leader is to find someone that you can confide in that you can empty yourself out. The Lord has prepared such a one for all of us. If we allow ourselves to go on like we are, then Satan will use our discomfort ness for his gain. He will often sabotage our hurts, and pains to bring us to a place of resentment, hatefulness and isolation. Because we aren't willing to open up and share our heart, we box ourselves in with our issues; sealing off all doors of opportunity by those located outside pain to come in and minister to us.

The job of a leader was once described as prestigious, so unique and pressing, that there be no room for hurting; and that pain and having feelings is not an option. We were told to suck it up and keep going; it's nothing but the devil, take it in stride. The fall of some leadership can be traced back when were broken and knew it and

BROKEN

won't do anything about it. We assumed our next sermon or bible study would ultimately self-repair us. It didn't but only covered up the real us underneath. We often played hardball with our emotions and feelings by ourselves until one day we actually strike out. While people's action in and outside of ministry will hurt and perhaps cause some form of brokenness, we all must rely upon the strength of God's grace to sustain and heal our sorrows. He will through grace, patch us up and then send us back out to ministry again and again. While it may not be your season to go through, but merely your season to recognize that you are damage goods. While I truly feel brokenness is a measuring stick to see how far we have gone. I also have come to believe that there is season in our lives were God will prescribe brokenness as a prescription to either slow us up or get our attention for our next assignment. I believe that if we are to truly walk in our purpose as leaders, the ministry of brokenness will arrive at the doors of our ministry unannounced. I believe with our hectic schedules of counseling, we need counseling too, whether preaching, we desperately need a word ourselves. I am saying to you right now that crying is not a symbol of weakness; but merely a device mechanism by which God will use to expose and recognize the areas in our lives in which we hurt. God will then send someone to minister to you and bless you.

The Prayer of Guidance

Father in the name of Jesus, help us to stay focus and ready to preserve the rights of thy word, to defend and uphold every word you have promise us. To forever declare your word true. To wait on you no matter the length, width, or breath of our trials, to not be caught up in the problems that come to close my God given vision down, but to find every means necessary walk in faith. Lord let vision not die, but become real for this life and the life to come. Refresh our hearts, empty our reservoir and pour a new profound revelation into our river banks of knowledge, validate us with your presence, Let your words flow again now with clarity and purpose. Lift the brokenness of our spirit and bitterness that we so wrongfully display from us. Let us not become quitters but finishers of a dream designed just for us. Help us to find hope in that which has been marked for our success. Let us not be weary in well doing, for we shall reap it if we faint not. As we lay by the brooks of what appears to be stale water, my soul longs for your instructions again, that we might move prayerfully in for me thy servant This I pray in Jesus Name

    Amen

CHAPTER SIX
STEP OVER IT, YOU CAN DO IT!

*O*ften when there is turmoil in our lives, we are slightly confused about just how we should address the situation. Do we stand and fight the good fight of faith? Do we rebuke the devil off our finances, our children, our bodies, and our circumstances? Do we enlist the support of our prayer partners to undergird as we stave off the attacks of the enemy?

When we find ourselves in a season of brokenness, it is there that we cannot rail against the will of God. Very often we are rebuking and binding what is not the devil, but the handiwork and design of God Himself. It is God that ordered our steps through the wilderness of brokenness so that he might cultivate the fruit of patience and temperance in us.

Once we've accepted that the path to the good life that God has destined for us may very well lead us through the wilderness before we get to our promised land, we must be careful to pay attention to the instructions given to us by our Father concerning each battle we face. There will be battles where the Father instructs you to war with the enemy with all of the strength that He has given. Later on in your journey, there will be battles where He instructs you to stand still and see His salvation.

The season of brokenness is not a place of defeat. It is a place of victory and triumph for those of us who will adjust our ears to hear what the Spirit of Lord would say to us. Hearing what God says and responding in accordance with it is crucial to experiencing true victory.

"Coming to the Battle Prepared to Win"

And they told him, and said, We came unto the land whither thou sentest us, and surely it floweth with milk and honey; and this is the fruit of it.

Nevertheless the people be strong that dwell in the land, and the cities are walled, and very great: and moreover we saw the children of Anak there.

The Amalekites dwell in the land of the south: and the Hittites, and the Jebusites, and the Amorites, dwell in the mountains: and the Canaanites dwell by the sea, and by the coast of Jordan.

And Caleb stilled the people before Moses, and said, Let s go up at once, and possess it; for we are well able to overcome it.

But the men that went up with him said, We be not able to go up against the people; for they are stronger than we.

And they brought up an evil report of the land which they had searched unto the children of Israel, saying, The land through which we have gone to search it, is a land that eateth up the inhabitants thereof; and all the people that we saw in it are men of a great stature.

And there we saw the giants, the sons of Anak, which come of the giants: and we were in our own sight as grasshoppers, and so we were in their sight. (Numbers 13: 27-33)

I want to add a bit of contextual background to the scripture that I just cited. This is a pivotal time in the history of the children of Israel. They have escaped from Egypt experiencing God's mighty hand of provision as He led them out of bondage into freedom. He has given them His law with which to govern themselves and He has promised that He would bring them into the land of Canaan.

At this particular time, Moses was instructed by God to send spies into the land to search it out. The promise that He had given the land into their hands was never in question. From scripture we can ascertain that He was clear before sending them into the land to spy it out that He would surely bring them into it. God's command for them to search out the land had everything to do with them submitting to His leadership.

Send thou men, that they may search the land of Canaan, which I give unto the children of Israel: of every tribe of their fathers shall ye send a man, every one a ruler among them. (Numbers 13:2)

God's instruction was for Moses to send men to search out the land of Canaan which He had already given to them. Yet, they allowed themselves to be intimidated by obstacles that appeared to be greater than the promise of God. Because of their unbelief, which the Bible refers to as an evil report, they were sentenced to wander in the wilderness for forty years. Their unbelief disqualified an entire generation from inheriting what God originally intended for them to possess. Indeed it would take forty years to weed out the rebellion, murmuring, disbelief, and doubt that made the children of Israel unfit to inherit the promise of God. It would be the generation that followed them that would actually inherit the Promised Land.

It is easy for us to look at the children of Israel and underscore their inability to receive the promise of God, but many of us are as guilty as they were. God has promised many of us an inheritance of health, wealth, and spiritual prosperity, but we will allow the giants of our brokenness to cause us to disbelieve what God has said. Instead of coming to the battle prepared to win, we allow bitterness, insecurity, and intimidation to convince us that we are unable to be victorious.

It is time for us to come to the battle expecting to be victorious. We must absolutely be convinced that it is our time to inherit the promises that God has ordained for us to receive. We must reckon that we are that Joshua Generation that will inherit the promises and no giants or walls of defense can stop us!

We must, with reckless abandon, trust that God is able to perform what He has spoken. We must hold onto that trust with a certainty that will allow us to look our circumstances dead on knowing that the difference between receiving the things of God and not is simply believing His report.

"Step Over It "

And he said, Hearken ye, all Judah, and ye inhabitants of Jerusalem, and thou king Jehoshaphat, Thus saith the Lord unto you, Be not afraid nor dismayed by reason of this great multitude; for the battle is not yours, but God's.

Ye shall not need to fight in this battle: set yourselves, stand ye still, and see the salvation of the Lord with you, O Judah and Jerusalem: fear not, not be dismayed; tomorrow go out against them: for the Lord will be with you. (II Chronicles 20:15, 17)

It is important for us to inquire of God exactly how adversity should be handled. As I mentioned before there is a time to fight and there is a time to endure. Knowing the difference between the two calls for the wisdom of the Lord which we must seek in prayer.

There are those times, however, when God Himself steps in and knocks the enemy flat on his tail clearing a path for us to walk through. It is in these times that we must simply learn to thank Him for the victory and step over those obstacles that no longer have the ability to block our path.

Such was the case with the children of Israel when they received the word that God was going to fight the battle for them. The only thing they could do was "step" into action and move forward beyond the obstacles of their enemies.

There are some stages of brokenness, that unless God steps in and clears a path for us we are unlikely to move ahead. God is faithful, and it is in those moments when you feel that you cannot make another step that He comes in and supernaturally influences your circumstances. It could be that you receive an unexpected check in the mail just as they are about to foreclose on your home. Perhaps a miraculous and unexplained healing takes place in your life as the doctor has given up on you.

What ever the case, we must be sure that when He does move in our circumstances that we aren't negligent to move forward. Bitterness and anxiety can often blind us to the fact that God has already removed all barriers to His promises. We have to call ourselves into action to step over those things that are already defeated and move forward into our destiny.

Step over your physical sickness and step into your healing! Step over your past and into your divine destiny! Step into your purpose, you can do it!

CHAPTER SEVEN
VICTORY IN BROKENNESS

A season of brokenness is not a place of defeat. It may very often be a place of refinement and pruning, but there is a clear path of victory to be extracted in this place of brokenness. Often we believe that because we are in a season of brokenness that we are to be decked out in sackcloth and ashes.

This could not be further from the truth. Our season of testing contains the ingredients that will propel us into the greatest victories of our lives. It is imperative for us to see it that way.

Pruning for Progress

There must be a cutting down first before a true harvest can be gathered. During our seasons of brokenness we must still sow if we want harvest. We must go through if we want to reap God's blessings in our lives. Being broken has a lot to do with pruning.

BROKEN

Verily, verily, I say unto you, except a corn of wheat fall into the ground and die, it abideth alone; but if it die, it bringeth forth much fruit. (John 12:24)

Your progress starts with pruning. Pruning can be defined as removing dead parts, improving shape and stimulating growth. I have found that in many seasons of my life, I had to get rid of old baggage before I could embrace the new things that were awaiting me. Because change is inevitable, growth should be anticipated. I believe that God wants to reshape us while we are in the pruning process. This reshaping will allow us to grow in better form and with direction. The pruning process will also rid us of unnecessary things that have been designed to choke our purpose.

<u>No pruning, No progress</u>

Pruning always deals with cutbacks. Ungodly things in our lives must be purged so that we can be pure vessels and available for the Master's use. God wants us clean and ready to be effective ministers. Failure to go through the pruning process will disqualify us from connecting to God's promise for our lives.

This is where I believe that Satan has a hidden plan. He endeavors to defeat the believer by making us think that the pruning process is God's way of punishing us. It is important to maintain your prayer life when you are going through. Every set back is not a defeat. Trust God and know that He is purging you to His satisfaction so that you will be ready for your harvest.

But in a great house there are not only vessels of gold and silver, but also of wood and of earth; and some to honour, and some to dishonour.

If a man therefore purge himself from these, he shall be a vessel unto honour, sanctified, and meet for the master's use, and prepared unto every good work.

Flee also youthful lusts: but follow righteousness, faith, charity, peace, with them that call on the Lord out of a pure heart. (II Timothy 2:20-22)

Progress can be defined as steady improvement. Just because you are in a storm does not mean that you are not progressing. When we find ways to journey through life's challenges, little by little we are making progress. This progress will not only help us to pass through those storms, but it will help us to complete what just might be a God given test. Don't throw in the towel now. Your progress depends on it.

Broken, But More Than a Conqueror"

Who shall separate us from the love of Christ? shall tribulation, or distress, or persecution, or famine, or nakedness, or peril, or sword?

As it is written, For thy sake we are killed all the day long; we are accounted as sheep for the slaughter.

Nay, in all these things we are more than conquerors through him that loved us.

For I am persuaded, that neither death, nor life, nor angels, nor principalities, nor powers, nor things present, nor things to come, Nor height, nor depth, nor any other creature, shall be able to separate us from the love of God, which is in Christ Jesus our Lord. (Romans 8:35-39)

BROKEN

The enemy is a challenger who fights below the belt with unauthorized tactics. Satan sees you as the underdog and he desires to take you out at any cost. The enemy's final blow is often made very apparent when things which have been working in our lives seem to speedily decline and our worth has depreciated. The enemy wants you to be miserable and embarrassed, but you must continue to declare that your loss is only temporary. God is able to restore all that you have lost in abundance.

Our ability to perceive God in our situations has a direct impact on our level of endurance. When we see God in our situations we are able to weather life's storms with more ease. If we are willing to let God be the captain of our ship, eventually there will be some smooth sailing even in the roughest tide. There is no storm that can rage against the calmness of His presence.

There will be times in your life when you may experience what seems to be an inundation of hardships. In my years of pastoral counseling, I have reminded many parishioners of the importance of keeping their focus on God. In many of these sessions it became apparent that the person had allowed people, issues and the like to pull them away from God. It is so easy to clearly see Him as our source when we are experiencing the constant rain of His blessings upon our lives. The challenge, however, is being able to maintain our focus on Him when we have entered a season of tribulation and the showers of His blessings appear to be no more. We must not empower anyone or anything to the point that they are able to separate us from Jesus Christ. Are other people in your life more important than Jesus Christ? It is very important that we nurture our relationships with family and friends, but we can not allow them to supersede the relationship that we have with our Heavenly Father. While my wife and I were engaged I gave her my military yearbook and in it I wrote, "I love you, but God will always be first in my life." Some may view this inscription as cruel and perhaps inappropriate, but it was very important to me that she be made aware of my position. I recognized God as my source, and I was not willing to compromise my relationship with Him under any circumstances. Regardless of how intense the problem is and how broken you have become, you must not lose site of your source. He is aware of everything that is going on in your life and He has already supplied every weapon that you will need to be victorious.

We must understand that when we attempt to fix things they are only fixed temporarily. Nothing that we fix on our own truly stays fixed. When we realize this and allow God in, He will do away with the patchwork and make us whole. Often times when we have been hurt, we put up personal barricades in an attempt to keep people at a distance. As a result, many people have learned to live with the broken areas in their lives. They have been doing it for months, some for years. In the eyes of society they appear to be functional men and women, but on the inside they are wounded and desperately in need of the Master's healing touch. We find great contentment in our home remedies for healing and it is only when we really get in the thick of things that we remember to call upon God to fix our mess. Thank goodness He is not like man, as we have the tendency to forget people that have forgotten us. God is ready to mend the broken areas in your life. You may be going through this very moment and still have not taken the time to seek the Lord. You do not have to carry this burden alone. You have been designed to be victorious. You are more than a conqueror. God understands your situation, and He will never count you out. In Him you are secure, having all of the provision that you will ever need. Let the Lord be your door to deliverance, your gate to freedom and your exit from bondage. Allow him to tear down those barricades of pain and fill your heart with joy and peace.

The Unspoken Thanks
By Jerlette Mickie

"A Poem written for those who forgot to say thanks"

Purpose: I wrote this for those who often feel as though there work doesn't matter and their service to others appears to go unnoticed. The anticipating success of your pupil shall serve as the everlasting mark you laid upon their lives.

Over the years you have serve the Lord
Reverencing the God you so humbly fear
Planting seeds in the life of thousands
While shedding a many of tears

Preaching with so much tenacity
Teaching with knowledge and experience
Sharing the Good news of Jesus Christ
Pressing forward with all perseverance

Catapulting potential leaders
To be the forerunners of every team
Teaching us to be responsible in life
While pursuing our purpose and dreams

Years of prophetic planning
Pouring into your daughters and your sons
Who are now changing the world because of you
Oh what a great job you have done

Your service is to be noted and commended
You always be consider, one of the best in the ranks
May these words bring joy and excitement?
To you my eminence, from the unspoken thanks

When sitting around pondering and reminiscing
Over a life prosperous and intact
Empowering, doctors, lawyers, teachers, common people
Who are now making an impact

Speaking into our lives early so that we could be sure
Using the Word to make us full and complete
Leaving a legacy prestigious and profound
A road model for others to repeat

Haven't heard from all of those you've empowered
Rejoice your eminence; you've already done your part
No matter were they go, or what they all shall become
They will always have your mark

CHAPTER EIGHT
BROKEN BUT THE VERY BEST IS COMING

I took this moment to write concerning the many ministries and ministers who ministry appears to be in a dormant status, left thinking this will never happen , this vision isn't for me, thinking their season has gone for ever. I want to compel you to get up from there and abandon your past. You can do this by promoting your future.

In spite of what has happen in our past, we must not fail in our efforts of petitioning God for greatness. We must not close shop and quit because of every uninformed test that has invaded our space to challenge us. We must journey through by talking to God and petitioning him for things that he has no doubt already wants us to possess in our live first place. Our families, our past life, our past situations must not dictate what is to happen to me now that I am under the umbrella of God's plans for my life. And if God has something for me , I must reckoned it so, by pursuing all which he has stored for my life. Jabez gives a great bold request towards

God. He is precise and to the point as to what he is asking for. It is apparent that he knows history, but he doesn't allows it to repeat itself, with the same results it wore on his ancestors etc. He leaves me the understanding that if I can serve the master, surely I can talk to him, and if he hears me, I believe he will answer.

I Chronicles 4:9-10 And Jabez was more honourable than his brethren: and his mother called his name Jabez, saying, Because I bare him with sorrow.

10 And Jabez called on the God of Israel, saying, Oh that thou wouldest bless me indeed, and **enlarge my coast**, and that thine **hand might be with me,** and that thou wouldest keep me from evil, that it may not **grieve me!** And God granted him that which he requested.

There are four things that Jabez prayer requested to happen

- ✓ **Bless me**
- ✓ **Enlarge my coast**
- ✓ **Thy hand be with me**
- ✓ **Keep me from evil, that it may not grieve me**

The book of Isaiah gives a close resemblance of Jabez situation, but here God is leading the charge towards spiritual prosperity and success.

Enlarge the place of thy tent, and let them stretch forth the curtains of thine habitations: spare not, lengthen thy cords, and strengthen thy stakes; (Isaiah 54:1-2)

For a moment let me focus on ministry experiences. I speak right now to leaders with Vision and purpose yet you have not witness fruitfulness in your season. Since God is no respect of person, we all must encounter our seasons. Every ministry that is divinely orchestrated by God shall encounter bumps and bruises, highs and lows, hills and valleys, quietness and turbulence, in route to fulfilling its divine purpose. It is a mere picture of Jesus assignment to secure our freedom. Our progress can be closely monitored by the way we thing while experiencing these challenges. Every Leader inserted by God is attached to that assignment as the helmsman or steersman to take that ministry through such a course, and though the journey is rigid, and full of uncertainties it is the messages for that city that will bring hope and keep the vision alive, renewing and keeping hearts fresh and focus. No ministry or leader designated by God can avoid such a trip. One must be very confident that the very best is coming.

There's no doubt there was a season where the church had no legs, couldn't go or take itself anywhere. Numb with no full movement, helpless to say the least, working on extended time, trying to make ends match up, Dormant in an arena where God called growth to be. Your resources are limited internally and are about dried up. It appears your source and provider has passed you up. Your praise is silent and it seems your worship doesn't event count. **And yet while the scriptures declare: God will never leave you nor forsake you, there is still this sad feeling while in waiting he left you for somebody else.**

Struggling to meet the heavy demands of ministry, you confront your adversary which your issues, praying for change, you get controversy, looking for away out you get stuck in it, expecting to go forward, you are held up, A simple call to God, No answer, The spirit of embarrassment shows up trying to make you quit what you said God told you to do. While the vision may seem clear, the thought of arriving there diminishes everyday. **While the scripture declare God will put no more us than we can better, it is apparent he knows my limitations better than I** There are times while we are making every attempt to continue, while the switch in our hearts are turning on and off, going through the motions, trying to follow your routine of service for his name sake. **While the scripture declares**

that the eyes of the LORD are upon the righteous, and his ears are open unto their cry. It just doesn't appears that there is a sign indicating that he is there at all times.

What you have offered to God seems to have been intercepted and or stolen, not counted for righteousness, seems you have been cutoff, disconnected and out of service, what was you only course of surviving has now been terminated..

The locus has been eating up your time, rendering your service null and void, leaving a false appearance as if you never gave God anything. Not a praise, not a worship, not a prayer, not an offering, nothing. Forever starting over, but really not having the grip you need to pull through it all. Let me say this; The very best is coming **This is often how it is in ministry, Jeremiah states his cry in the matter:**

Jeremiah 8:22 is there no balm in Gilead; is there no physician there? why then is not the health of the daughter of my people recovered? He is saying here, Where is my recovered, where is my help.

I want to let you in on something; The **Very Best Is Coming:** this a new day, and a new beginning. Job 8:7 brings this prophetic Word even closer: Though your beginning was small, your latter shall be greatly increased.

- ❖ **Thought:** Winners are not created with a stack deck; they are created through adversity with all odds totally against them. They emerge to the top, because, there opponent left them down in a pile unattended and forgotten.

Don't let the season's mess up your celebration, or halt the festivities, take a glance back where you came from, your storms, your trials, your issues, your hurts, your pains, your disappointment, if you look where God is taking you too, you would throw your own party.. If you quit now you will miss it all, for sure everything else is ahead. Just remind yourself these words: I see my future and I like what I see.

The devil weapons are devices of distraction; if he can get you focusing away from your divine assignment he can have you chasing the wrong things.

Everything you've gone through or is going through even right now, is pushing you closer to the place God is ordering you to or have destined for you to be at I had to go through this: I was ordered through this, I was ushered through it.

Greatness is produced from trials and test, persecution and separation Oh yes God had to separate you in order to preserve you for this season. You couldn't hook up, hang with, or even depend on nobody but him. Got wants to showcase you, He is the one that has all bragging rights, Celebrate, and give a shout out to him; for the best is yet to come. Isaiah continues on with this timely instruction.

Enlarge the place of thy tent, and let them stretch forth the curtains of thine habitations: spare not, lengthen thy cords, and strengthen thy stakes; Isaiah 54:1-4

3 For thou shalt break forth on the right hand and on the left; and thy seed shall inherit the Gentiles, and make the desolate cities to be inhabited.

4 Fear not; for thou shalt not be ashamed: neither be thou confounded; for thou shalt not be put to shame: for thou shalt forget the shame of thy youth, and shalt not remember the reproach of thy widowhood any more.

Chapter 54 comes in from the heels of an prophetic proclamation, rendering us a Snapshot or preview of the crucifixion of Jesus Christ

BROKEN

to be in chapter 53: From these profound scriptures we are given hope, because of what Jesus would eventually endure for us. **Isaiah** writes these words with inspiration and urgency, telling us to get ready, get in position because the Very Best Is Coming. It all starts win Jesus.

We must not be afraid to expect the inevitable, while thinking the impossible. Asking God for big things is only in his sovereign nature to release it. But when he declares a thing, expect it right then and there.. Something small is what we can reach everyday. God operates with provision for the present and the future. The call to enlarge must forever be apart of our thinking process as we see ourselves in lieu of greatness.

God has a way of preserving us with his creation: Genesis declares that he made the ocean, the fish and the fowl of the air, when God allowed Jonah to be swallowed up: the truth of the matter he was not punishing him as much as he was sheltering Jonah in order to harness his investment. We are at some places in life because that is where God wants us at that time, perhaps where he can take ownership of our thoughts, knowing that destruction may be at our door, he calmly arrest our emotions.

Enlarge: expand the space were you are to where you are expecting be, your thinking; make room, open wide, and make space in your thinking**.**

Stretch forth and widen every bit of your faith into believing that it will become impossible for you not to get it. To the point that your way of thinking is embedded in seeing a promise become a reality. Isaiah is saying get ready, God has something for you and it is so big, bigger than you, yet it is for you,

He continues by saying the past has had its purpose, but your future is already appointed: and look not in dismay, but in great anticipation for what is next for your life.

It is vital for you this day to speak into your life and tell yourself over and over:

The Very Best Is Coming: In spite of: what is happening, what's been said, what's been done, The Very Best Is Coming: to give you back your, ministry, marriage, job, your family, your, finances, to hand over your stuff.

Get up, The Famine Is At Your Back and God is rendering you favor over your famine years. God is going to change the time, the process, and the procedure.

What's coming is better than what's been, if it's yours, take it, if not leave it a lone, but never the less, keep going, the wind is at your back. Everything God promise, everything he spoken, everything he passed to you, was not a mistake, you are not dreaming, you're not in denial, but your are in the season now where your delays has become a demand. Your famine has been attacked by your favor, for what was in front of you to mess up your vision, is now behind you It is important that you have a positive approach to your destiny. It is coming here, it is coming to me, prophesy to your self, according to thy word….

The kind of turbulence that came to sell you short of your destiny, Winds of destruction, packing havoc, chaos in your marriage, chaos on your job, chaos with your children, damaging winds coming to revoke your anointing, strip you of your true worship, true praise, to take your breath away, take your dreams away, to run off with your vision. What was happening to you, happen but you held in there, you must now take a moment to have a: Thank you Jesus Fit, Halleluiah Fit, Worship Fit:

And though it may appear that the devil has knocked you back a couple rows, a couple of lanes, pushed you off the track, trying to disqualified you, violated you, trying to arrest your purpose for existing,

Wake up, open up your eyes, for the wind is at your back. Wake up, wake up, you are about to role up on a blessing, you got to come up out of this. You are destined to be a blessing.

Whatever you lost back there, you must believe that you can get it back by going on ahead.

If you would take the moment to access your storms we would gratefully find out that these storms mean us well, if we learn from them all. For example; consider this thought:

Storms that push us forward indicate we aren't where we should be, for we have gone far enough to appreciate the ultimate favor of God. Storms that push us back, is an indicator that we have gone ahead of God, and he is just bringing us back to the place where we can commune again with him, to where he is. Storms that push us from side to side, is an indication that we are not moving, so he bring some turbulence in or lives to shake us up to stay focus and to eventually move us forward. Being still can cause you to doubt your whereabouts in Christ Jesus.

CHAPTER NINE
THE WINDS OF CORRECTION

I stated earlier that the wind is at your back, and you are going to be just fine because God is going to see to it that you arrive. God is putting his favor on your famine To devour the enemy for your sake, to restore your barns, filling it up to plenty and giving you back your identity and your purpose.

Exodus 10:19 And the LORD turned a mighty strong **west wind,** which took **away the locusts,** and cast them into the Red sea; there remained not one locust in all the coasts of Egypt.

God is sending a wind of correction, which would identify your hindrance, removing it from you, and then casting it into the sea. The wind of correction comes to give you favor over your famine, peace over your storm, victory over your battle, that you might finish the race. God's plan in your storm experience is to caused you to be fruitful in the land of your affliction. Praise God, that's right, there is no storm that can stop him from putting treasure in your sack.

Since the very best is coming, the lack is getting ready to vanish, your shortages are coming to an end, the waiting is over, no more delay.

Psalm 118:9 The Lord was my stay…………………..was my grace, But God extended my time.

Declare it today, right now at this very moment: **I AM COMING UP OUT OF THIS.,,**

You can sit there if you want to, and weep over your past and present errors, over your issues, over your fault, when God has made a way of escape. Don't get me wrong, the famine is coming in the land, but your house shall be save, your stuff shall be kept, your children spared, because it is pertinent that you survive this season for the blessings that await you in the morning. Isaiah makes it plain and real:

Isa 40:28 Hast thou not known? hast thou not heard, that the everlasting God, the LORD, the Creator of the ends of the earth, fainteth not, neither is weary? there is no searching of his understanding.

29 He giveth power to the faint; and to them that have no might he increaseth strength.

30 Even the youths shall faint and be weary, and the young men shall utterly fall:

31 But they that wait upon the LORD shall renew their strength; they shall mount up with wings as eagles; they shall run, and not be weary; and they shall walk, and not faint.

Isn't it funny that when you don't need help, help is everywhere, but when you get in trouble there seems to be no help? Although we may have insight of a break through that is coming in our life, don't forget the people that helped you, the people that brought you out, helped you over it, less a **FAMINE** shall come on thee again.

Acts 18:9-10

Then spake the Lord to Paul in the night by a vision, Be not afraid, but speak, and hold not thy peace:

10 For I am with thee, and no man shall set on thee to hurt thee: ***for I have much people in this city.***

It is so important to know that the work of God serves as a reminder to many of us that, when the wind is in our face, and all kind of things are blowing at us, God is able to bring us through it all.

"Turned On, Tuned In And In touch With God"

Over the thirty-two years that I have confessed Jesus Christ in my life, I have had not one problem that kept me from straying or straddling the fence. The truth is I've had many problems and obstacles to come and shift me from my divine purpose. It is critical that you have an ongoing relationship with God, that is that you stay tune in, turned on and in touch with him daily. There are some journeys that you are going to take, that only he can get you there or even bring you through it.

The more we confess Christ in our lives no matter how many years it's been, we are tried, proven, and test in every areas of our lives. Our time in service means nothings if we just count the years and not the cost. It cost a lot to follow Jesus, the right way. It cost a lot to follow his blue print right and not detour from it.

It would be nice if our titles and position paid off for us wouldn't, just for a moment, if this was possible what would you ask for in exchange, what would purchase for your position, for your title.

BROKEN

I am constantly asked this question. Where Am I supposed to be? What am I supposed to be doing? Many people, who have and still are asking those questions are sincere and honest, concern about there future. though ,while it is not wrong to be asking the Pastor or a friend, we must all understand that there is a procedure and sequence for petitioning God

In all of my years, I have never seen as many Christians back then as I do today who require so much maintenance, needing so much repairs, and yet think they are straight with God because they come to church.. They check in with the church, with the leader and resume there forgotten place in God. They have no idea where they are in him. They expect the leader to know that, they expect their best friend to share that; they are expecting prophecy today to keep them in line. There is a difference of being at church and having church.

When you seek after the heart of God , when you are desperate enough to want him in your life, when you cry and wail for him, when you choose to summons him in your life daily , when you , not somebody for you, but when you inquire, he is careful to respond.

In Chapter 10 of St. John, he is declaring that my sheep hear my voice, and they follow me , they believe and follow, they obey, the problem here is you are claiming to be my sheep and not believe and obey, The reason you don't believe is because you are not my sheep.

Message Bible

Scripture: St. John 6:35

The person who aligns with me **hungers** no more and thirsts no more, ever. Will not be left out in the dark, but kept up to date. Praise God for his favor.

It cost friends, love ones, old associates, it cost your life………..
it cost personalities, but to God be the glory, The greatest pain I believe that is in life is when someone that you have been sharing your life with, just gets up and walk off, and leave you shaking your head and holding the pieces of your heart together, the ones that appeared to be so close but really so distance from you.

I believe that we should invest double in to God what we invest to others. As long as we hang around in this life, for any periods of time we must stay committed and focus in Christ, if we want any real peace. The enemy knows that people can cause you to loose your joy, loose your patience, loose your peace, loose your mind, loose your focus, that at this point it doesn't matter what your title, or your position is, if you really want a change, you got to believe the very best is coming. While you have decided to re assess your situation, one must consider these thoughts:

New Living Bible

He **who comes** to me will never go hungry, and he **who believes** in me will never be thirsty.

Amplified Bible

He who comes to **Me** will never be hungry, and he who believes in and **cleaves to** and **trusts in** and **relies on** Me **will never thirst any more** (at any time).

It is not about gaining ground on God, that is absurd to think one can, but it is all about timing, God's timing and our obedience to his timing.

While church may be a place for some to exercise and flex their spiritual gifts, for me it is really about reporting back to God and rendering due respect to him. Gathering together to reflect and celebrate on what he has already done, and expecting him to

BROKEN

do tomorrow. But when we make our walk with God personal, it requires a more direct question as it is relates not to his favor but my place. It is not about where I ought to be, where I suppose to be, or where I should be, I know how to get hyped up, I know the moves now, the hook ups, I even know the way the Jones do it. But what I am experiencing is me talking and he not responding, what I am coming to recognize is that I may not be where I think I am at. I may not be all of that and a bag chips, just a couple of kernels popping every Sunday, with little impact even on myself.

The imposed petition should be: Lord Show Me Where I Am Maybe I didn't do it right, I was cute with my praise to the point I don't even believe what I am saying, have I become arrogant with my worship that I think that I am fit for thy kingdom.

How can you do ministry without doing service, Tell me how can you expect a harvest in thy kingdom and you aren't real sheep; Thy gift shall make room for thee.

We must be careful to not think that we have crossed all of our t's and dotted all of the I's while saying things like:

- **Surely I must be close,**
- **I sing, I play, sometimes I perform**
- **I work in the church 24/7**
- **I got connections, I know people, people know me,**
- **Surely I must be close**
- **They like me,**
- **Surely I must be close**

Quote: You are as close as you what hear, who you are hearing, and who you are obeying.

The key to understanding where you are, **is what you are willing to hear, who you are willing to hear it from, and who you are willing to obey.**

THE WINDS OF CORRECTION

There is a conspiracy against my salvation, there is a pulling in my spirit, a nagging on my anointing to miss my true purpose for existing. I am budgeting out my walk with Christ, for everyday counts and is crucial to my survival, therefore I have just enough to keep me together and just enough to tell somebody Jesus saves. I can't hang with my past, I can't hang with my issues, I cannot afford to hang wit my guilt trips. I refuse to no longer kill all my joy, kill all my praise, disqualifying me to come before his presence, because when I am around myself, speaking negative to myself, I have nothing to bring and nothing to say that will summons the father. With God's very best at my door, I will not miss my purpose any longer.

We are living in the season of vast opportunities, and great wealth, people are tapping in to these opportunities, at every chance they get, they no longer wait for the hand of God, or the voice of the Lord, they no longer pray for it, they no longer touch and agree, they no longer, seek the guidance of the holy spirit, but trying to gain it all on your own can cost you your life. Wealth, and riches can put your salvation at risk; can disqualify you from ever reaping a true harvest in your life.

I don't know about you, but I need him more today than yesterday, you can act like you got it together, I don't have all together, what I use to depend doesn't work an longer. I must look to Jesus. He has the very best for me.

Watch what you are attaching yourselves to, and what's holding on you, you can become vex just by the wrong company making themselves to comfortable around you. They leave you stranded with their negative agenda, causing you to veer off from your purpose all together.

Nothing has really change concerning Satan's strategy, there are more obstacles than ever to bother us, hinder us , more carnal things,

BROKEN

things that focus on us than on God, things that feed our carnal man, things that puff up our flesh man, things that recognized the man and not the God in us. The more we put the focus on ourselves we loose our God given direction as to where God is in our lives. It is important that we stay close to Jesus. Every now and then when the race gets so hard to run, and it will, it has, we must slow down the pace of things and just say. **Jesus Keep Me Near The Cross..** If it seems like we just want to throw in the towel, and we sometimes do, whisper: **Jesus Keep Me Near The Cross. Although we a re broken at times, we must find the way and will to talk to God. When nobody is listening, he is, even right now.**

Coming Out of The Shadow

I Samuel 16:1

And the LORD said unto Samuel, How long wilt thou mourn for Saul, seeing I have rejected him from reigning over Israel? fill thine horn with oil, and go, I will send thee to Jesse the Bethlehemite: for I have provided me a king among his sons.

2 And Samuel said, How can I go? if Saul hear it, he will kill me. And the LORD said, Take an heifer with thee, and say, I am come to sacrifice to the LORD.

3 And call Jesse to the sacrifice, and I will show thee what thou shalt do: and thou shalt anoint unto me him whom I name unto thee.

4 And Samuel did that which the LORD spake, and came to Bethlehem. And the elders of the town trembled at his coming, and said, Comest thou peaceably?

5 And he said, Peaceably: I am come to sacrifice unto the LORD: sanctify yourselves, and come with me to the sacrifice. And he sanctified Jesse and his sons, and called them to the sacrifice.

THE WINDS OF CORRECTION

6 And it came to pass, when they were come, that he looked on Eliab, and said, Surely the Lord's anointed is before him.

7 But the LORD said unto Samuel, Look not on his countenance, or on the height of his stature; because I have refused him: for the LORD seeth not as man seeth; for man looketh on the outward appearance, but the LORD looketh on the heart.

8 Then Jesse called Abinadab, and made him pass before Samuel. And he said, Neither hath the LORD chosen this.

9 Then Jesse made Shammah to pass by. And he said, Neither hath the LORD chosen this.

10 Again, Jesse made seven of his sons to pass before Samuel. And Samuel said unto Jesse, The LORD hath not chosen these.

11 And Samuel said unto Jesse, Are here all thy children? And he said, There remaineth yet the youngest, and, behold, he keepeth the sheep. And Samuel said unto Jesse, Send and fetch him: for we will not sit down till he come hither.

12 And he sent, and brought him in. Now he was ruddy, and withal of a beautiful countenance, and goodly to look to. And the LORD said, Arise, anoint him: for this is he.

13 Then Samuel took the horn of oil, and anointed him in the midst of his brethren: and the spirit of the LORD came upon David from that day forward. So Samuel rose up, and went to Ramah.

The Lord does not look at the things man look at; God looks at the heart, .The heart of man is the real you. There are some things that you may not qualify for, but God has a away of changing the prerequisites so you can be pick, so you can be next.. It has nothing to do about you, it is about his glory, his reputation for blessing or validating you.

When Samuel looked around to picked a King to rule over Israel, it was from the last of Jessie's seed, (David a shepherd boy)the youngest son, not develop, not fully instructed, others are before him, others have paid there dues, others have work they way to be next. David by all order is not next, but last.

You have worked hard 9-5 for somebody else to shine, somebody else to get promoted, you have tidy the sheets, swept the floor, for somebody else to excel, and it looks like you are in the rear unnoticed, unappreciated, not respected, hurting and feeling violated. You have all the qualification of a servant's job, always following, always getting instructions, always getting orders, Maybe you are a shoes salesman, car salesman, stock clerk, secretary, nurse, waiter, waitress, ball boy, serving in one area or another, Take this moment or season to learn your job and the job in front of your job, One day or you will come from behind the scenes and take your divine assigned place . Whom God desires, he will equip for every good work. One must be;

- o   Ready to be lied on in order to be blessed on

- o   Ready to be not liked and still make a difference

- o   Ready to start from the rear and treat it as the place where God is showing you the big picture.

- o   Ready to not be recognized and still impact your surroundings by the service

You render.

God is getting ready to bring you to the forefront, by requiring more of you with him. In your quiet time, in your prayer time, in your study time, He is molding you through hurts, through setbacks, through misfortunes, through mistakes, through the issues of others, so when you come from the rear, you can go forward and arrive without stopping. You won't make the mistakes of your mothers, your fathers, your sisters, your brothers, your pastors, your, Sunday school teacher, your music director, your, first lady, be cause it was back in the shadows of not be important, not being used that your where able to see some stuff and not go spiritual blind. God is giving you the new meaning of survivor,

"God's been watching you during your shadow experience"

Jeremiah 1

⁵"I knew you before I formed you in your mother's womb. Before you were born I set you apart and appointed you as my spokesman to the world."

⁶"O Sovereign LORD," I said, "I can't speak for you! I'm too young!"

⁷"Don't say that," the LORD replied, "for you must go wherever I send you and say whatever I tell you. ⁸And don't be afraid of the people, for I will be with you and take care of you. I, the LORD, have spoken!"

⁹Then the LORD touched my mouth and said, "See, I have put my words in your mouth! ¹⁰Today I appoint you to stand up against nations and kingdoms. You are to uproot some and tear them down, to destroy and overthrow them. You are to build others up and plant them."

It's not hard to find the next leader if you look in the right places. Check the leftover section from the church, check the overlook section, review the serving area, check the altars, the praying room, the crying chapel, stop by the intercessory room, check the janitors room, check the nurses station. Leaders are birth through servitude. If you are not in charge, maybe that's a good thing, you will get there through your profound love for others.

What others said you weren't going to be, you'll be that and much greater, What others said you won't have you'll have that and much more.

Greater Works..................................

John 14:12-15 .12 Verily, verily, I say unto you, He that believeth on me, **the works that I do shall he do also; and greater works than these** shall he do; because I go unto my Father.

13 And whatsoever ye shall ask in my name, that will I do, that the Father may be glorified in the Son.

14 If ye shall ask any thing in my name, I will do it.

15 If ye love me, keep my commandments.

You are getting ready to come from being that duck in the pond where nobody has been paying you in attention, to that Swan in the lake, your anointing will direct attention.

A diamond in the ruff, wheat surrounded by tares, before I could react he called me, before I could respond he sent me, before I could justify myself he ordained it so, It is nothing we've done to deserve anything, just the grace of God. Serving will prepare you to being served; David soars from a servant to a king, Joseph advances from the pit to the palace, and Job advances from rags to riches.

CHAPTER TEN
YOU WERE CREATED A WINNER

$\mathcal{N}$o matter how you feel even right now, I want you to know right now that God created at you to be a winner. Understanding our seasons of being broken, we too must move forward and grasp the lasting moments of victory, the last days of our purpose. I must remind you that God intentions for you have not and never will change.

Genesis 12:2-3 And I will **make of thee a great nation**, and **I will** bless thee, and make thy name great; and thou shalt be a blessing:

3 And I will bless them that bless thee, and curse him that curseth thee: and in thee shall all families of the earth be blessed.

The transition from the world to the church can be devastating to say the least, particularly if the motives are not right, it is liken unto an ill-prepared relationship, from the single life to the married life, don't kid yourself, there is a difference. *One must be prepared and committed to serve God, and not rely on the past provisions of life to make it. Your future depends on your willingness to trust*

him and obey his command While there are so many obstacles, diversions, infraction, altercations, and unnecessary roughness going on, nothing is fare, it is either right or wrong, nothing is maybe, it is either okay or not okay, The past may have roughed you up so, that it appears your present isn't no better, but you **have a future**, with Jesus, While there are an enormous measure of uncertainties, there is one thing that still stands in tact, God commands a blessing for your life, God commands healing for your life, God commands deliverance for your life, God commands peace for your life, God commands wealth for your life. He is certain he will preserve you for his use.

Business adventures, investments, stock market, 401, all have had their share of success and failure. But God made a covenant with: one of your forefathers, you weren't born again to be defeat, he has made a covenant with you, you have every bit the right to be bless as Abraham. Shout Glory. Everything around you might, give up, quit, slow up, slow down, but you just wait on God, but you just thank him in advance, because **you are going win this battle, you are going to win this race.**

While we put a lot of effort into competing, we must redirect such efforts into completing our assignment with the confidence that Christ Jesus can bring. Any chance of surving comes through him.

Hebrew 6: 11-15 And we desire that every one of you do show the same diligence to the full assurance of hope unto the end:

12 That ye be not slothful, but followers of them who through **faith and patience inherit the promises.**

13 For when God made promise to Abraham, because he could swear by no greater, he sware by himself,

14 Saying, Surely blessing **I will** bless thee, and multiplying **I will** multiply thee.

15 And so, after he had patiently endured, he obtained the promise.

You were created to succeed, to keep going, not to stop, not to rest in the land of weariness, The Apostle Paul writes: I press towards the mark, saying: I am after something, and that is to no my purpose and place in the body of Christ. To be all that Christ called or summons me to be. With God you have a future and it is promising.

And though it hurts, keep going, it can be distracting, but keep going, The Lord is saying "I have empowered you with tough love"................

St. John 14:18 I will not leave you comfortless: I will come to you.

Message Bible: I will not leave you without help as children without parents. I will come to you.

Genesis 12:2-3 And I will make of thee a great nation, and I will bless thee, and make thy name great; and thou shalt be a blessing:

3 And I will bless them that bless thee, and curse him that curseth thee: and in thee shall all families of the earth be blessed.

It is impossible for you to loose, when Christ has secured your victory, you need to walk in that testimony, shout in the victory that has been established for you, through the blood of Jesus.

John 16:7 Nevertheless I tell you the truth; It is expedient for you that I go away: for if I go not away, the Comforter will not come unto you; but if I depart, I will send him unto you.

It is in your birth nature, or born again nature, that you go through, but to the promise, for your victory is connected to your suffering.

BROKEN

Luke 10:19 Behold, I give unto you power to tread on serpents and scorpions, and over all the power of the enemy: and nothing shall by any means hurt you.

Get up from there, there is a bright side to this, it's getting better, there is a promise out there, with the resources to see you through, and his provision for us is connected to it.

"A MOMENT WITH GOD"

Have you ever gone to the doctor's office because you where complaining about how you felt and that you want to feel better, the doctor comes in and say, now tell me from a scale 1-10 how is the pain, what are you feeling right now, and what is the one thing on your mind, going through your head. Can you walk, walk for me….

While cleaning out the actic of my mind, I have found that my titles mean little to my situation, and if I could turn them in for something else, it would probably go something like this.

I would ask for a supply of bandages for the many scratches that constantly occur while comforting people, and rubbing shoulders with people out to hurt me.

A **neck bracelet** to keep on me so I won't let any one, or situation turn me away from my focus., nor stir me away from my purpose, drive me away from my destiny.

A **dripping wet towel** to heal the wounds I receive daily just trying to do the right thing, I would ask for **a tourniquet** to stop the bleeding from the cuts I receive when my back is turn, I would ask for a **plate of your finest revelation**, that I might be ready for the next hike.

For I have given it all out; Lord I need a new supply I would ask for new strength, to not wrestle anymore with people, but to put that new strength into the saving of real souls.

I would ask for **shelter right away,** for those that are around me, in the huddle with me, that really don't have my vision, t keep me focus.

I would ask him to dried my tears, for deep down with inside of me, I cry, day and night I cry, I would ask to for clarity concerning my storms, is this really happening, or am I having a dream.

I would ask for peace like a river, the peace that often evades me when I need it the most.

I would ask him to not let me die, before the vision is birth, and the mission is fully accomplished. I would ask for a fresh revelation to drink that could travel through my heart, and re-warm the areas of my soul that still long for thee. I would ask for after visiting the sick, empowering others, impacting their lives. Lord send a raven by to not only feed me but patch me up, I look fine outside, but the truth, I am hurting from within and I need you to hide my nakedness, I am broken, with the parts that praise thee, the voice that worship thee, the feet that followeth thee, the eyes that look for thee, the heart that panted for thee, battered and torn, send a word unto me Lord, send a message unto me, send a note unto me, send a messenger unto me. Maybe you are feeling like this, and want to address God. It is perfectly okay to speak to him and let him know right now what you are feeling.

CHAPTER ELEVEN
BROKEN THROUGH PARENTING

$\mathcal{W}$e often have a lo t to say about somebody else's situation, rendering our opinion, our advice that no one probably cares, and our judgment that no one asked for. When we are faced with a dilemma concerning those close to us, we tend to go hush hush, we want it concealed, and we want it; quiet please. We appear to be quiet ourselves, but the truth of the matter, is we are angry. We tend to blame ourselves. We say things like, I raise them up right, they went to church, and they sang on the choir, I just don't understand, what am I going to do. I pray that this small insert that I have written on parenting can help.

Your daughter or son, comes in and wants to chat with you, maybe go out for some ice cream, and then they say first, promise me you are not going to get angry, you rest your spoon on the table, you are sitting straight up and while your eyes are looking directly into there's, they say: **MOM, DAD I AM PREGNANT, I GOT THIS GIRL PREGNANT. Does this sound familiar?**

BROKEN

While I have never, during the raising of my children had to experience teenage pregnancy. I have counseled many parents and their children on such matters in the twenty-two years of pastoring. My only daughter whom I always cared for with unfeigned loved really took care of herself. I tried most of my life sheltering her from boys and what I called bad company. We were a family that just centered our life on church. When my daughter had chosen to be with other people, I frowned, fussed, complained, had a fit, got angry, even stayed up until the clock ranged, the door open, she came in, looked okayed and then only then I would go to bed. I would wake up and purpose myself to talk with her about her friends. I would say, hey just talk to church folk, often threatening her about being with the wrong group. She would reply; please Dad I am not doing nothing, I know. We would get into short arguments, until one day my daughter sat down with me and gave me her personal feelings her life, not mines, she shared with me that she new the way of God, and that mom and I had raised her well, and how I should allow her to live her life. Sitting there angry inside, I cried within because, I had tried to live life for her and with her, trying to protect her every movement. I later realized, I was trying to do more than just be an example. I was hiding the world from her. I eventually realized it was best for her to meet new friends even outside of church. I became confident that my daughter could maneuver utilizing the tools and principles we had taught her by the life we lived. My daughter has since gone on in life to meet the man of her dreams, who too is an inspiration to my life, and who has given me a new breath of fresh air (smile). While this is not the overall outcome of many families, it is not the end.

As parents I realize that while we are not always right or wrong, we must always have a two-way communication with our children. In doing so to, we all can avoid some valley experiences that may be too deep to come up out of.

BROKEN THROUGH PARENTING

The father of the prodigal son in the bible taught me a great principle and valuable lesson, that no matter what my children think of me, or what they do in life, where they leave and go to, they will always be my children, Always. This principle is a fact that will never change. While people change names, they cannot change who they are, or the seed from which they came out of.

I f you are a parent of a teen-ager who is now pregnant getting ready to have that child, I would like to first speak to your hearts.

While it is devastating to know, that your baby is having a baby, it is equally devastating to know, that your baby knows nothing about of raising one. You need to arrest your emotions and feeling about being embarrassed about your family name, title or immature excuse. We all were living a life of embarrassment until Jesus found us. That child need you right now more ever in life, not the Pastor, not the saints, not Auntie Betty, or grandma, but you. We make so many errors in life that goes undetected, and think that we are problem free, that is far from the truth, As a Pastor, I have had to counsel parents on the brink of loosing it all together, because of what there children decided to do. Where do you go from here, do you say, that's there problem, you made your bed, sleep in it, I am not talking care of that baby, you bet not leave school, you need to get a job, is that dead beat father going to support it, you bet not keep that baby, you know what the bible says about abortion. Where do you fit in all of this? This may sound like small talk, but the truth is it is hog wash, and pathetic to the ears of those knowing their role in parenthood.

Our dreams have always been to provide security to our children, until they are grown and able to work, and have their place like we do. When circumstance come to alter all of this, we must not renege on our responsibility to help our children, you see no matter what choices they make in life, good or bad, they will always be our children. Coming up in life I was a hard liner to the above things I am saying now, because I sheltered my children with a stiff arm and practically order them from those areas that I felt posed a threat to there future and minds. The truth is that there is danger in sheltering them from experiencing things for themselves. I remember asking God to keep them out of harms way, when I was keeping them myself too. We can sometimes hurt, rather than help.

As we allow space after teaching them instead of preaching to them, they will respond I believe in a way that will make you forever so proud. I am proud of my children, they have blessed me, and just to see the life they have chosen. While our teenagers may be minor in age, they are not in character or personality. The teenagers of this age have learned the ways of life quicker and faster that those of our youthful days, as children who have been abuse, thus becoming defiant to the common rules of life that surround them. We as parent have a say in, what our children will be, and do as a minor and later as an adult. The preview of this is shown in how we care for them in there adolescent years.

In some of our churches, the age ratio is so off when trying to get children to play together, or just interact. Some are left with no one to relate to their needs, so they look elsewhere. As parents we must not get lazy because of our hectic schedules, from work the gym and church. Remember our legacy rest in the hands of those we raise and educate. They will remember not just what we told them, but also what we taught them It would behoove us as parents to not provoke our children to wrath, but to being successful in life, caring and responsible. How communication with them is precious and should not lead them to doing bad things for spite, for revenge, reverting to bad choices after being raised in the home where God is the governing authority, granting us grace and mercy. While many children have no daddies, it is more to it than saying, I have done all I can do. Is it, the child by law is still a minor and still our responsibility, yes there are something's that would just make you down right angry, but that's my child, Ask God to give you strength to not only cope but understand.

We must preserve all the rights to see our children turn it around and have a future as good as ours. We must show our concern and our support in raising our grandchildren. Sadly speaking some of us, knows our children by name only, we fail to talk, communicate, and we are only good for responding and reacting what we disagree with. Stop blaming yourself for your children actions. If you failed in the past, get it together at this present. Work with there errors of life and help them to lead a blessed and righteous life through Christ Jesus. Stop holding there past before them; you must be available to be there for them. It is not a time for them to be lonely, separated, and scared of succeeding. All parents served as covering for there children and the devil knows this. The very thing the enemy enjoys is when trouble comes in our families we fail to stick together and work it out. You may have mouthed you children in the company of others, trying get your selfish point across, but I declared unto you this day, that God is not please, and you will answer to God for the potential jewels, diamonds and rubies he gave you to help polish, that may have been destroyed in rough. Get back in there and see your children through those hard times, particularly until they are of age (adult) to be release. We must then release our children to live a full life of responsibility and accountability no longer to you, but to Christ Jesus. Amen

CHAPTER TWELVE
SERVING MATTERS THE MOST

Quite often when controversy, and misunderstanding comes, it leaves a residue smeared with wrongful thinking and unwise decisions. With careful craftiness and deceitful skill, the first approach of the enemy is to impress upon you to discontinue serving in the church. You have been hurt, nobody loves you, you are a lost case, nothing matters anymore; this is far from the truth. Satan comes during this period of time while you are down and out and going through, to make sure you never get up again, by stripping you of your desire and willingness to serve. I will attempt to share a small portion in this chapter to just give you a word of advice: that your worship and willingness to serve in the kingdom has gotten you this far.

In spite of all your valley experience, and disappointing days, nothing should keep you from rendering a service in the kingdom of God.

The greatest example of a servant was Jesus:

Matthew 20:27-28 27 And whosoever will be chief among you, let him be your servant:

28 Even as the Son of man came not to be ministered unto, but to minister, and to give his life a ransom for many.It is safe to say: to serve is to be Christ-like.

"When one serves he introduces God through our humiliation and through a willingness to be humble. You should never allow yourself to be so broken that you cannot serve; after all that's what Satan wants. Are you going to give him what he wants? I mind you he doesn't want your serve, but he wants you to stop serving his number one enemy God."

While what you do blesses the church, makes the pastor to look good in the eye of visitors and other members, it may even cause your friends to appreciate you. The end results are that it is for Christ sake that we serve each other. Your service pleases God.

If we are expecting to make it through these rough times, we must keep serving and don't give a second though about quitting. I have learned over the years that the journey to leading is by way of serving. When we dismiss the God given thought of serving we jeopardize our ability to be humble, and meek. God understand that through serving we find our purpose. When you choose not to serve, you are merely saying, I am bigger than God, who served all his life.

While we are yet going through, serving has a way of putting our flesh under subjection to his will for our lives., merely because serving takes the focus off of us and place it on the kingdom. If we are to gravitate to this concept then the thought is: *"It Is Not About Me"*

Serving deals with time: specifically when it is time you don't have. Serving requires giving of yourself.

While the Bible portrays an array of people who served: King David who was a notorious worshipper, he also was a servant: for he served Saul in spite of his; life being threaten. It apparent that if you do the right thing, the right things will come back to bless you every time.

While everybody is called to serve one another, everybody will not serve one another for various reasons. I come to accept that there are five reasons: **PRIDE, POSITION, POWER ,PREFERENCE & CIRCUMSTANCES. Whenever we allow these areas to clog our judgment to serve, we have invited the adversary in also to sabotage our chances of survivor .**

The sooner we serve, the quicker you will be in his perfect will and in position to be served. When you serve others you serve the master.

If we wait to be served then there is evidence that we have no intentions of serving. You will encounter people with all kind of stories about what happen to them in church, at home, on the job, on the highway, in the groceries store, at a sale; whatever and however you view it, It will not release you to the comfort zones of your life. There is no excuse to have somebody else's excuse for not serving. While there conversation may be tainted with a host of negative words to follow; you must keep serving in the kingdom.

Don't loose your serve..

It is important to make this point; while serving is a choice of your will, it stands as a cleansing tool for God to chisel away the rough edges of our self-inflicting attitude about life.

While God desires more than ever to bring you out and into a land flowing with chances and opportunities, make no mistake about this; he will not promote or a cause a celebration on anyone who is not willing to serve. Everyone must have a prayer life, that serving others is an honor, despite how others feel about serving.There are those that you will meet that come charged up to come in the house of the Lord, while others will show there expressions of discontent way before sitting down, there body language indicating they don't want to be here. While everything is happening to you and you loose your position, it's okay, and you loose your title it's okay, and if you loose friends, that's okay too; Don't loose your willingness to serve. In the kingdom of God.

CHAPTER THIRTEEN
RESHAPING OUR FRAME
TO FIT HIS WILL

God loves us in so many ways that he will everything he can to display that love towards us. All through the bible he portrayed that love to a point that today our lives have been transformed by his unfeigned grace and mercy. Because of what Christ has done for us leaves to believe that even in state, brokenness is also another conduit for God to reshape our frame to fit his will. While it al doesn't fill great, the finish product will matter the most.

Let us read up on Jeremiah the prophet.

The word which came to Jeremiah from the LORD, saying,

2 Arise, and go down to the potter's house, and there I will cause thee to hear my words.

3 Then I went down to the potter's house, and, behold, he wrought a work on the wheels.

BROKEN

4 And the vessel that he made of clay was marred in the hand of the potter: so he made it again another vessel, as seemed good to the potter to make it.

5 Then the word of the LORD came to me, saying,

6 O house of Israel, cannot I do with you as this potter? saith the LORD. Behold, as the clay is in the potter's hand, so are ye in mine hand, O house of Israel.

Implication: The Potter, he was fashioning(transforming, framing) a vessel, and it became marred (disfigured, spoiled) in his hands. It wouldn't yield. The clay has to be just the right texture (.quality, consistency) So he pitched it aside. Then later he picked it up and made it into another kind of vessel. In the process of waiting forte clay to settle or to yield could came back to it and proceeded with his divine purpose.

Note: From our main text: there are two things we want to see: that is 1. the power of the potter, 2. the personality of the clay

Yield- give way to, give in to, give up to , submit to , capitulate (surrender)

Thought #1: There are people or circumstance that God is not able to repair. God can do anything but fail. The quicker we catch this long -standing principle; we will become wise to call on him. The potter knows what he wants before he creates it, so he is not interesting in moving quickly but ensuring that whatever he creates will serve it's purpose. He is not necessarily concern about the flaws we initially display; because he is able to reshape us at anytime in our life upon our request that will ultimately please him. People who are sophisticated and hardened in sin, it is difficult to get them to listen to the Word of God, or moreover yield their will to God. Often times when we are broken and in despair we become stiff, uninterested, and not willing to understand. What God has in mind for us will not spring forward without your will being broken. When we refuse to yield to God the issue, the problem, we tie God's hand to produce the goods for our life. Being angry, disgruntled, mad or embarrassed will not fix your situation. Listening to God, to who he sends in your direction, obeying the father's instruction, is what will free you from your bondage. Regardless how gifted we think we are when it comes to dealing with stuff, it would serve us well if we had a spirit of submission whereby if we are willing to allow God to invade our circumstances. He would do just for us. It is apparent the he would never do anything against our will. I love the verse of scripture below that helps me in my times of despair.

2 Timothy 2:20 But in a great house there are not only vessels of gold and of silver, but also of wood and of earth; and some to honor, and some to dishonor.

21 If a man therefore purge himself from these, he shall be a vessel unto honor, sanctified, and meet for the master's use, and prepared unto every good work.

Through this spirit of submission we are able to cleanse our thoughts and our hearts for a new beginning. Whenever God comes in ; he refreshes us. We find that we are able to live out our life the way God expected it to be lived. Allowing God to come in; it places us in position to be used at will for his glory..

The Power of the Potter

We find in Genesis: God is Ultimate Potter, for he took clay and formed man of the dust of the ground, and breathed into his nostrils, the breath of life, and man became a living soul. Genesis 2:7

God is Self-governing: He is Supreme;

He has supreme power over the clay (soil), and that power is unrestrained
No soil can stop the potter
Nor can it questioned his right, or alter his plans
The soil cannot speak back to him

-The clay on the potter's wheel cannot get up when it wants to
-The clay on the potters wheel cannot talk back or react differently than what is was created for.
-The clay on the potter's wheel is not able to do anything
   - It can only yield to the potters hand

God has power to carry through his will
He answers to no one
He has no board of directors
He has no voters to whom he must respond
He has absolute authority
He is a God

The Apostle PAUL writes :

Romans 9: 19 Thou wilt say then unto me, Why doth he yet find fault? For who hath resisted his will?

20 Nay but, O man, who art thou repliest against God? Shall the thing formed say to him that formed it, Why hast thou made me thus?

21 Hath not the potter power over the clay, of the same lump to make one vessel unto honour, and another unto dishonour?

The Personality of your frame

We all start out clay (formless, shapeless soil, (no form) lifeless, and more than ever evident; we are incompetent (hopeless) and incapable of doing anything for ourselves. If God is makes us, then we must be still without shape or form, so he can shape us into his image, giving us form. Since clay has no form, we too can stay that we if we refuse to submit to his authority through those he has given power to govern over us. In a season where we may be broken; we must never leave from under the umbrella of authority or spiritual covering attempting to obey our emotions.

While we sometimes forget who we are and who's we belong to; The Scriptures confirms this; **Psalms 103: 14** For he knoweth our frame; he remembereth that we are dust.

When we receive the inspiration of the scriptures we receive life with expectation. Understanding that we may be broken, God's Word come to restore and deliver us, to the place he has ordained. He reminds us again and again that where we are is far better than where we was. Below is some additional scripture to pull us from our amnesia experience.

Ephesians 2:1 And you hath he quickened, who were dead in trespasses and sins:

12 That at that time ye were without Christ, being aliens from the commonwealth of Israel, and strangers from the covenants of promise, having no hope, and without God in the world:

Apostle Paul Speaks to the Romans

Romans 5:6-9 6 For when we were yet without strength, in due time Christ died for the ungodly.

BROKEN

7 For scarcely for a righteous man will one die: yet peradventure for a good man some would even dare to die.

8 But God commendeth his love toward us, in that, while we were yet sinners, Christ died for us.

9 Much more then, being now justified by his blood, we shall be saved from wrath through him.

You and I need to know again

    a. God is a sovereign God
    b. We are clay
    c. We were dead in trespasses and sin
    d. Without strength
    e. God is the Potter with power

Romans 9:16 So then it is not of him that willeth, nor of him that runneth, but of God that showeth mercy.

When our situation has gotten so bad, we sometimes desire not to do anything but sit and cry it out. Nothing is right, nothing is working, nobody appears concern, and you

During my Career in the military, I have had some great moments serving my country. I have been around the world stationed in various countries. My most challenging experienced however came while being deployed to the Republic of Vietnam in late October of 1975. I had joined the military for various personal reasons, to only find myself heading to war. My heart melting with just the thought of going, being as Vietnam during that period was in a unrest state with the United States. As we were deployed over the waters for several months. I found myself crying from within, upset with the military and with God. Why me God, why me. My overseas experience challenged me to trust God, and depend on him. It was never easy until I read the word of God, and decided to trust God.

Although I gave my life to Christ, I still felt lonely, and captivated by my own personal emotions about not only going but just being there as well. I said all of this to imply these thoughts: There shall be times when you are going feel isolated because of your circumstance, but be encourage that you as I did can overcome every obstacles by believing in yourself. In the middle of foreign waters, I am left to cry to God and to depend on his grace and divine mercy. We spent many days and night, sitting in the middle of the ocean waiting to either attack or be attacked. Nevertheless I was relieved to know all of this drama would soon past over. Thank you Jesus. I said all this to send consolation to you, that no matter where we are, God will be there also. I had just recently received Christ in my life, but yet fear had gripped me. The fear of dying before my time; dying perhaps a terrible death disturbed me in the worst way. I met another marine on the ship and we talked about the goodness of Jesus Christ, and how is a keeper and a protector. I can recall saying I need to hear that man, he replied; you also need to believe. I asked him to pray for me, he replied lets pray for each other. There is a lesson here that every believer should note. There are going to be some valley experiences that only you will be able through Christ to bring your self out of. In spite of what is being told to you, you must believe. My friend would tell me it is all about the basics, pray, read, make melodies in your heart about the God you trust and depend upon. After thirty-two years of ministry, I have come to accept this to be true; that every time I put my trust in Christ, he never fails to come and shelter me with his unwavering love. Never think your situation is so bad that it is not repairable; even if you are in the middle of nowhere experiencing brokenness; know that you can summons God through faith and he will come.

You Haven't Lost It All

I recall in 1987 when I was release from active duty because a grave sickness, I was given thirty days to relocate from military housing, after being told two week prior you have been medically discharged effective in thirty days. I panic because I hadn't gone house shopping at all. My wife agreed that we pray for God's help and direction. Within two weeks we had a place to rent in Jacksonville North Carolina. What I thought was challenge turned out to only be the beginning of numerous testing of our faith. When I was abruptly discharged, my pay drastically decreased where as I could only afford to rent the house and practically nothing else. We didn't see this forth coming, matter of fact it blind-sided us. From that period everything was either getting behind, late getting out or not able to meet the obligations. Battling with a sickness that suggested I don't do much activities and my wife looking for employment. Leona was determining to find some form of employment to help meet the needs around the house, as it was getting crazy around here. I recalled one day my wife had job applications laid out all over the kitchen table. About four months later I recall a recovery agency came to our door to retrieve (repossess) our car that was three months behind. It hurt so badly during that period because we were 12 payments from paying off this car. I was threatening to give up on everything and everybody; but all along my wife encouraged me trust God for he knows. So my and I kids watched in dismay as our Cadillac Deville rolled away from our house. It was hard not to think about what was happening to us and as the man; I accepted all the responsibility of our newly found problems. It had gotten so bad, that my initial issue about my sickness could not compare to the welfare of the entire family. I care not how I was fairing, but my concerns were on my family needs not mine. While during this period I pastored a church, I received no salary or commission, and concealed all personal matters from the church. I recalled weekly helping people stay afloat in their personal matters, while mine was drowning. I recalled crying like a baby in my study, asking God, am I cursed, why is this happening to me, what have I done Lord, I cannot take this anymore. I did not receive an answer in my angry state. As time continued, we had lost employment, lost our first car, rarely paying our rent. I recall loaning our car to one of our members to take care some family matters, one week day morning this car was totaled. We were down now to no cars and had to rely on others to pick us up and take us back. It was crazy. Finally our rent began to get behind as we try to juggle the funds from my medical retirement to meet all the needs. The lights is being turned off, the water is being shut down, the heat is being cut off, . We get one bill caught up only for another to go behind. We lived on a twenty-nine day plan; that was to not let anything get behind thirty days. Unfortunately our credit was so bad we could not get a loan for a biscuit. We were not just a risk but also a danger. It got so bad that we were pawning everything to meet our needs, even down to my wedding ring, stereos, and televisions. During the 1988 period up unto June 1989, the sheriff visit us monthly to give us an eviction notice, but somehow the rent was paid before our fifteen days to vacate. God's grace and mercy live in our house. I had never cried in my life as much as I did during that 1987-1989 era. What hurt so bad, I was a man and fought to avoid showing my emotions. The military had taught me to be tough, stiff and stern. I have found through Jesus Christ you haven't lost it all. He is our shield and strength for hard times like the ones I experienced. I am a living witness today that you too can make, when all your trust and hope is in The Lord.

Provoking Your Purpose To No End
(keep your dreams alive)

Here are just a few nuggets that I have used in the past to keep me going while dreaming. It is a danger to dream and not eventually moving forward in what you are dreaming about..

> ➢ *Understanding that the vision is to you first*

> ➢ *Developing a plan that will achieve the goals of that vision*

> ➢ *Release your understanding with a mission statement*

- Keep pursuing your purpose until you arrive

- Understand you have been ordained for this season

- Release the hidden joy of knowing God called you to do this

- Use your remaining joy to change the atmosphere around you

- In order to survive you must be an innovator

- Your first covenant begins with you agreeing on your calling

- There must first be a level of trust in God's guidance while going through

- There must be a strong conviction that he will pull you through it all

- Develop relationships God that will help you accomplish the mission, by

- connecting to him all by yourself

- No matter what, when, where, why and how things happen don't quit

Broken Still Calling Your Name
By. Dr. Jerlette Mickie

This Song is about being broken and yet still determined to call God for help and guidance through some of the most trying times of ones life. It is a song that determines to ask the master if he hears us, to answer, and if he see us, to come and shelter us because we are broken with no comforted insight of being repaired

Verse 1

As I filter through the rubbish
Of my broken heart
Wondering what went wrong,
How it all fell apart,

Oh Lord I am broken,
Holding the pieces, that remains
Hoping to get another chance
As I call on your great name

Verse 2

The winds of life comes blowing with no notice at all,
Packing winds of destructing coming to compromise my call,
But as I hold to your promise determine not to fall,
Saying Lord if you cannot see me, can you here my call

So I summons my master
As I keep my focus aim,
Saying Lord here I am broken
Calling on your name

Chorus:
Calling your name, calling your name
I need to hear from you; I need a word to take me through
Calling your name, calling your name
Because I am sitting here broken, sitting here broken,
I am sitting here broken calling your name

BROKEN

Verse 3

From the wind and the rain
Come the hurt and the pain
The heart felt rejections
Seems like there's no protection

As my voice begins to shiver,
I cry to God thy giver,
to come and see about me
to come and see about me. (octave change)

Calling your name, calling your name
I need to hear from you, I need a word or two
Calling your name, calling your name
Sitting here broken, sitting here broken,
Sitting here broken calling your name

Repeat Chorus : Calling your name, calling your name
I need to hear from you, I need a word or two
Calling your name, calling your name
Sitting here broken, sitting here broken,
Sitting here broken calling your name

With so much to say on those trouble filled days
In a life so unspoken because my hearts been truly broken
Re assessing all of my past, how long will this all last
Gripping with the facts, Gripping with the facts

What can I say when my day is in a disarray
And no matter how much the light appears
The hope just seems to just disappear
And I am left with all these fears
And unstoppable, unstoppable, unstoppable te……………..ars

Repeat Chorus: Calling your name, calling your name
I need to hear from you, I need a word or two
Calling your name, calling your name
Sitting here broken, sitting here broken,
Sitting here broken calling your name

Eight Motivational Scriptures

(A Healing Remedy for Brokenness)

Find these passage of scriptures in the Bible; and write in your own words what you feel is motivational and inspiring to you about these scriptures. If you know of more scriptures add them to this list.

Job 1:8

Job 2:9

Deuteronomy 28:14

Psalms 34:19

Jeremiah 3:5

Psalm 91-3

Psalms 118-18

Psalms 121:1

The Seventeen Most Deadly Weapons that will lead to Failure

I have listed at least seventeen causes of failure in ones life. This is by no means the causes of failure. I encourage you to list additional causes of failure during your study allotted study times.

BROKEN

Procrastination

Not being responsible

Not being accountable

No vision

No purpose

No goals

The wrong crowd

No Budget

Disobedience

No prayer life

Doubting You Can Do It

No Patience

Jealous of Another Man's Treasures

No focus

Ones Perception Is Off

Not Avoiding The Same Traps

Your excuse out number your goals

Closing Remarks: While our society is taking on new shapes and images, it is certain that nothing remains the same; everything is changing around us at us. Because of the uncertainties that often awaits us; we must be declaring that God is our source for all recourse, and our ultimate vision for the provision. I pray that this book has informed and inspired you to go forward and finish what God started in you. While every situation has a purpose, it takes certain qualities to fulfill our purpose. Ambition need to sit high above our list of things to possess. Ask God to grant you the tenacity to do what others have dared to perform. Although you where not counted in the number to win you, you won. Ask God to grant you continued strength for every season of your life, that even after you have gone through it all and done his will, you will be found yet still standing on the pieces than remain and still work.